North Carolina: Race of the Century

Harvey Gantt vs. Senator Jesse Helms
Issues vs. Loyalty

Tony L. Powell

Ambassador Press, LLC

in the spirit of excellence

Columbus Ohio

North Carolina: Race of the Century
Harvey Gantt vs. Senator Jesse Helms

Copyright © 2006 by Tony L. Powell

Published by Ambassador Press, LLC
P. O. Box 722, Reynoldsburg, Ohio 43068-0722
Email: ambpress@insight.rr.com
http://ambassadorpressllc.com

Cover design by Imagine! Studios
http://www.artsimagine.com

ISBN 0-9787850-0-2
LCCN 2006933285
First Ambassador Press hardback printing: September 2006

Dedication

This book is written in loving memory of my mother, Bessie Lee Powell, and my late brother, James Roger Powell, and my grandfather, Matthew Powell, for their wisdom, caring Christian values and dedication.

I also want to express my appreciation to my sister and brother, Janice Powell and John Powell, and to my aunts and uncles, nieces, nephews, and cousins and the entire Powell family.

I am also grateful for my many teachers, college professors and friends who supported and encouraged me.

Tony L. Powell

Table of Contents

Chapter One

Since the beginning of the American journalism tradition, the powerful influence of mass media coverage on political issues has been most evident throughout the United States. Most notably during the years of the 1820's through the 1860's the role of the American press changed as a result of political and technological developments. These years were also crucial to the development of the reporter as a professional. For example, in the beginning of the 1820's, reporters accounted for about one story in ten, but by the end of that period reporters were responsible for one in five.

On the contrary, editors had a more active role in terms of reporting their viewpoints in newspapers. Editors accounted for between 13% to 25% of the stories in the early years between 1847 and 1860. As noted by many historians, newspapers were very political throughout this period (Shaw 1981, p. 49).

In terms of news dominancy, New York and Boston emerged as forerunners, with news filed less often from the South and West. For instance, both the West, in particular, and the South heavily depended upon the North for "Yankee products", such as colleges, commercial houses, Yankee ships, and, of course, news.

According to noted researcher, Donald Shaw, one of every six stories was launched from a Northern newspaper. Furthermore, Shaw stated that news often arrived in an abolitionist package sent to Southerners by steamships. Later years, however, railroads and telegraphs greatly enhanced the ability of newspapers to obtain and disperse information rapidly, particularly Northern newspapers.

In viewing the press' response to the growing audience of the 19th century, Shaw found that newspapers collectively did not alter their styles of writing during the 1820's through 1860's. Shaw stated that stories were just as "difficult" or "simple" to read at the beginning and end of the period.

Moreover, the contemporary press has continued to prosper (economically) as a result of the "penny press" concept. Cable devices and fiber optics have offered the American press institutions ample chances of reaching a more diverse audience. In light of the dominancy of those political stories of the early years and even today, it has become more difficult for press institutions to address some of the more pressing needs of society.

Lewin stated that the extent of American political, economic, ideological, and technological influence in the world in terms of saliency was evident in press coverage. He further posited that American media's selection of "news" stories was based on the values of media institutions and gatekeepers. American gatekeepers' needs and expectations in terms of "news" and "race" were embedded in American culture and values. In other words, the communication process was a part of cognitive relationships and ideas specific to the culture (Lewin et. al, 1964, p. 84). Moreover, Schramm noted that mass communication in any human society was controlled by cultural and group self-interest and by cultural expectations. Schramm further noted that American mass media reporting was a conduit through which individuals defined their views of the world and reinforced their values. Hence, it was too simple to assume a global village in which everyone's needs and values merged toward an American norm. The political and race conflicts between and within cultures were real, and the media illuminated that reality (Schramm, 1964, p. 83).

Shaw and McCombs (1972) noted that in political campaigns, candidates were viewed by information and images in the mass media. The information and story composition in the mass media were only variables many voters used in the decision-making process. Thus, newsroom staff and editors shaped voters' political reality.

Review of Literature

In the case of Tarheel Blacks (North Carolinians) in general and Black politicians in particular, the newspaper coverage of Blacks was historically displayed with negative connotations. Those negative connotations became a part of the social processes of reality for editors and the populace. Hence, the psychological and social devastation of White and Black relationships was covered by media institutions in their coverage of reality. More specifically, the impact of the media conveyed the ideology of the status quo which influenced the mainstream and suppressed the minority (Schramm, 1964; Megwa, 1989, Gandy and Barber 1990; Matabane, 1988). Kassajean's (1973) study indicated that Blacks were depicted as inferior and second-class citizens in comparison to whites.

Of course, the depictions were under the auspices of newspaper owners, executives, and gatekeepers. The ideology of journalists' coverage of Blacks was deeply rooted in traditional system values (Schramm, 1964, p. 83). The extent of that ideology was prevalent in the Harvey Gantt and Jesse Helms senate race. Chaudhary (1980) proposed that the portrayal of Black and white representatives was viewed differently. She noted that headlines were usually biased;

9

however, the size of headlines was usually the same. Most importantly, however, Chaudhary (1980) found that over a seven-year analysis of nineteen major metropolitan daily newspapers, Black elected officials had more negative coverage during political campaigns than whites. Gandy and Barber further noted that the mainstream press coverage of Black politicians was described with negative adjectives toward their personalities and behavior. Rowan (1976) found that several African-American representatives were victims of inaccurate press coverage. Rowan noted that Adam Clayton Powell, Shirley Chisholm, William Clay, Mervyn Pynally, and Ralph Metcalfe were viewed as bribers, drug abusers, and thieves. In Jesse Jackson's 1984 and 1988 presidential bid, mayor Marion Barry's arrest, and Harvey Gantt's bid for the U.S. Senate, the press's negative biases were further substantiated in their coverage.

Graber (1984) further noted that newspapers served as a conduit for voters' biases. Hence, the history of inherented biases and misrepresentation locally or nationally caused major political problems for Blacks and Black political aspirants. In fact, this type of negative misrepresentation coverage reinforced mainstream values and biases about Blacks and Black political aspirants which the press perpetuates. Thus, the press's misrepresentation set the agenda for mainstream white traditional voters by race (Kassajean, 1973; Chaudhary 1980; Rowan, 1976; Graber, 1984; McCombs and Shaw, 1977).

Statement of the Problem

From the inception of journalism in general, and North Carolina newspaper press coverage of slaves in particular, Blacks were victims of character myths, political domination and image distortion. In fact, the press served as a conduit and reinforced traditional values and shaped political reality for traditional mainstream populace in North Carolina. More importantly, the North Carolina press tradition was intertwined with its historical identity problem with the assimilation of Blacks within the political systems. Clearly, then, gatekeepers were part of the same economic and political culture which resisted Black assimilation. The impact of gatekeepers' decisions was further extrapolated by McCombs and Shaw, who posited that political news was a by-product of news organizations, and its impact was a by-product of gatekeepers' placement of news items (McCombs and Shaw, 1972). Thus, they believed that the placement of such articles had salience for readers. In other words, readers' assessment of politician's attributes--race included--was in direct correlation to the gatekeepers' decision-making process.

Specifically, the press serving as a conduit and gatekeepers as decision makers were powerful actors in terms of the social and political processes which created reality for readers. Thus, these individuals' values were interwoven within the organizational function of mainstream media institutions. Importantly, this construction of news by gatekeepers gave readers a distortion of reality; and philosophically, readers were inundated with dominant group agendas and values (Megwa, 1989; Tuchman, 1978; Fishman, 1980; Matabane, 1988; Fromm, 1947). Tuchman (1978) further posited that gatekeepers created a mirage of images through which Americans viewed their political leaders, and information became a repository of knowledge for readers in making and shaping their views about a candidate (Tuchman, 1978).

Of equal importance, other researchers further noted that gatekeepers familiar with the media's strategic mechanism, not only determined the news but also set the agenda (Megwa, 1989; Weaver and Elliott, 1985; Turks, 1986; Gandy, 1982; Becker, 1982; Megwa and Brenner, 1988b). In regard to white male senators setting news agendas and political agendas, Graber, 1984; Weaver and Wilhoit, 1980 found that seniority and committee position constituted substantial news coverage.

Contrarily, noted scholar Lillian Bell (1973) discovered a dearth of information regarding scientific literature and mainstream

11

coverage of Black politicians. Bell's study from 1960-70 found that in Baltimore, Cleveland and Atlanta, white newspaper coverage of a Black politicians increased if the editor felt he was a prime winner. The editor then served as a decision-maker for the amount of news coverage a politician received. Bell's study was important in the way that it was implemented in 1970 because thirteen Black politicians won U.S. Congressional seats.

Ironically, since Bell's study, the political climate, political race stratagem, redistricting, negative race coverage and media coverage of dishonest Black politicians have imbued the social and political fabric of our society. In fact, the negative press coverage has created problems for the electability and legitimacy of Black politicians.

Minority news makers have been handicapped with the utilization of the media in transmission of genuine issues (Megwa, 1987; Megwa and Brenner, 1988b; Paletz and Entman, 1981; Weaver and Elliott, 1985; Hess, 1986; Parenti 1986; Turk, 1986; Mueller, 1973; Poindexter and Stroman, 1981). Equally important, both the national press and the press in North Carolina have created negative political images of Blacks; and Chaudhary (1980) noted that political images of Black and white candidates were diametrically different because of race. Historically, the race factor in North Carolina and negative mainstream newspaper editors' coverage of Blacks were significant factors during slavery and throughout the 1900's.

Thus, it is important to examine how race issues and mainstream newspaper coverage of Harvey Gantt and staunch seniority senator Jesse Helms affected the United States senate race between the two in 1990. The following questions were formulated to guide the study:

1) To what extent did coverage of Jesse Helms and Harvey Gantt differ based on their race?

   1b. To what extent did coverage of perceived electability of Senator Jesse Helms and Harvey Gantt differ?

1c. To what extent did coverage of Senator Jesse Helms and Harvey Gantt's issue-oriented campaign differ?

1d. To what extent did coverage of perceived power of Senator Jesse Helms and Harvey Gantt differ?

1e. To what extent did media coverage of North Carolina's perceived values of Senator Jesse Helms and Harvey Gantt differ?

1f. To what extent did media coverage of Senator Jesse Helms and Harvey Gantt's North Carolina heritage differ?

2) How did Senator Jesse Helms and Harvey Gantt's agendas compare in terms of the favorability of coverage by the media.

3) To what extent did media emphasis on Senator Jesse Helms' and Harvey Gantt's integrity and honesty differ?

Significance of the Study

The subject of this study was chosen to contribute to a more scholarly examination of media impact on politics. Hence, the theoretical framework for the study was developed to examine and raise some fundamental questions and concerns about mainstream media portrayal of minorities in politics and Harvey Gantt's and Jesse Helms' U.S. Senate race in North Carolina. Some scholars noted that the composition of a news organization and individual's behavioral characteristics played a key role in setting a news organization's agenda (Paletz and Entman, 1981; Weaver and Elliott, 1985; Hess, 1986; Parenti, 1986; Turk, 1986; Megwa and Brenner, 1988b). Of equal importance, the interconnectedness of some political actors with mainstream news organizations and their skillful approach suppressed others' lack of such affiliations and skills in setting the

13

news media agenda (Weaver and Elliott, 1985; Turk, 1986; Hess, 1986; Linsky 1986; Megwa and Brenner, 1988a; Bennett, 1988).

More specifically, then, African Americans, in general and African-American politicians, in particular, were virtually incapable of permeating mainstream news organizations in setting news media, public and policy agenda (Mueller, 1973; Bernstein, 1981; Gandy, 1987; Poindexter and Stromm, 1981).

Moreover, the paucity of such research devoted to African-American politicians and aspirants and press coverage reveals the need for further assessment studies. (Chaudhary, 1980; Conyers and Wallace, 1976; Gandy and Coleman, 1984; Dates and Gandy, 1985). Kurt and Gladys Lang (1981) further posited that more research should be conducted to render a more lucid picture of press portrayals of political leaders and their influence upon voters and political systems. Clearly, then, the dearth of research on press portrayal of African-American political leaders or aspirants (nationally, statewide, or locally) setting the news agenda for voters in mainstream media in North Carolina gave credence to this study under investigation.

The significance of this study, therefore, lay in its manifest content examination of the *Raleigh News and Observer* and the *Charlotte Observer's* analyses (through May and November) of U.S. the 1990 U.S. Senatorial race between Harvey Gantt and Senator Jesse Helms. The influence of such a powerful North Carolina political figure as Jesse Helms and his conservative values and newspapers gatekeepers' value system concept were critical factors in determining whether Harvey Gantt (liberal) received favorable or unfavorable coverage. Hence, the linkage of past powerful white politicians in North Carolina proved to be interwoven in the fabric of the major mainstream newspapers which misrepresented African-American politicians. Equally important, the 1990 senate election campaign coverage by the *Raleigh News and Observer*, located in Raleigh (the state capitol) and the *Charlotte Observer*, located in Charlotte (the largest city in North Carolina) attached labels to Harvey Gantt and

14

Jesse Helms in terms of race, professional, and personal associations as well as competency toward solving issue-oriented problems facing North Carolinians.

Finally, the relevance of this study shed light on the history of mainstream press coverage and inherited structural biases towards African-American political leaders with race as a variable for legitimacy.

> Communication, taken as a whole, is incomprehensible without reference to its political dimension, its problems, and cannot be resolved without taking into account political relationships. Politics, to use the word in an "elevated" sense, has an indissolveable relationship with communication (UNESCO's International Commission Report, 1980:18).

The relationship of politics and communication was further posited by Chaffe:

> The world of politics and techniques of mass communication have intersected in fundamental and fascinating ways... The difficulty most thinkers have had in coming to a unified interpretation of communication and politics is exemplified by Thomas Jefferson, who once wrote, 'were it left to me to decide whether we should have government without newspapers, or newspapers without a government, one should not hesitate a moment to prefer the latter' (Chaffe, 1975:13).

Limitation of the Study

Consistent with most scientific literature on media coverage of African-American political leaders in general and media portrayal of African political leaders in North Carolina in particular, there was a scarcity of literature on local, state, federal office holders and

15

aspirants. Most of the research conducted on African-American political aspirants was national. In North Carolina, the total population constituted 6,333,000 and the total voting age population was 475,100. More specifically, African-American populations constituted 1,393,000 or 22 percent of the total population. Moreover, the total population of African Americans of voting age was 998,000. The total number of registered voters was 3,041,000, and the number of African American registered voters was 579,000.

In terms of federal officers, North Carolina had eleven Congressional districts. The second District (Durham) had the largest percentage of Black residents, 40 percent; First District (Cape Hatteras) constituted 35 percent of Blacks; Third District (Goldsboro) and Seventh District (Charlotte) 23 percent respectively; Sixth District (Greensboro) had 21 percent; and Fourth and Eight Districts (Raleigh and Salisbury) had 20 percent. Blacks occupied seats in the General Assembly for both Senate and House of Representatives. In this study, however, Harvey Gantt was unable to lure enough statewide white support for the United States senate office. This study was based on the United States senate race and coverage by two mainstream newspapers of Democrat Harvey Gantt and Republican Jesse Helms from May 1990 through the November 1990 election.

Two newspapers were selected for this study based on their proximity in the state of North Carolina; the *News and Observer* located in Raleigh, the state capitol and the *Charlotte Observer,* located in Charlotte, the largest city in North Carolina.

Methodology

This study will analyze seven months of newspaper coverage.

Additionally, it will analyze coverage by two mainstream newspaper of the Harvey Gantt-Jesse Helms race for the United

States Senate. The study will cover a period of seven months (May - November), using the manifest content analysis method.

Content Analysis: A Research Methodology

The importance of content analysis in communication research can bring highly reliable results if content analysis techniques are used objectively, systematically and quantitatively in analyzing manifest content (Stempel, 1981:119-120).

Communication scholars consider content analysis as one of the most important methodological tools used in conducting communication research. Among scholars there were various definitions of content analysis. For instance, Krippendorf (1980) posited that content analysis was a research methodology for making replication of studies and drawing valid inferences from data to their context. Kerlinger (1980) defined content analysis as a method of studying and analyzing communication data systematically, objectively, and quantitatively in measuring variables.

Kerlinger further noted that the systematic means undergirding the communication research study must be analyzed according to consistent rules. Additionally, Kerlinger noted that the sample selection must be administered with each variable being selected equally for analysis. Moreover, Kerlinger noted that the content analysis evaluation process was systematic; and the coding process was operated with uniformity. The term objectivity, noted Kerlinger, meant that personal idiosyncrasies (biases) of the principal investigator were not part of the communication study with the content analysis approach.

Thus, the operational definitions and rules for classifying variables were lucid and comprehensive. Moreover, if the communication study were replicated with the same content analysis approach, then the same results would occur. This quantification process allowed researchers to analyze results with statistical methods and report them with greater parsimony (Kerlinger, 1980; Dominick and Wimmer, 1987, p. 166).

Berelson (1952) provided a classic definition of content analysis methodology. He maintained that the key to understanding the utilization of content analysis and implementing it lay in fully understanding the meaning of objective, systematic, quantitative, and manifest content. According to Berelson, content analysis was viewed as follows:

> Objective... means the opposite of subjective or impressionistic. Objectivity is achieved in a content analysis study by defining the categories for replication purposes. If content analysis is subjective instead of objective, each researcher would have his own content analysis. Thus, objective means that the results depend upon the procedure and not the analyst.

> Systematic... means that a set of procedures is applied in the same way to all the content being analyzed. Second, it means that categories are set up so that relevant content is analyzed. Finally, it means that analyses are designed to secure data relevant to a research question or hypothesis.

> Quantitative... means recording the numerical values or the frequencies with which the various defined types of content occur.

> Manifest Content... means the apparent content, which means that content must be coded as it appears rather than as the content analyst feels it is intended (Berelson 1952, p. 18).

Finally, Stempel noted that there were four methodological problems that a researcher must confront in undertaking a content analysis study: selection of unit of analysis, category construction, sampling of content, and reliability of coding (Stempel, 1981).

Summary Organization of Study

The power and influence of the United States' mass media coverage on political issues became intertwined with the American journalism tradition in 1704. Through a selective process, constrained by organizational, social and cognitive factors, the news media constructed the framework within which individuals, groups, organizations, and cultures perceived social reality. As a result of this frame of reference, these individuals inherited the philosophy, values, and attitudes of the dominant groups in society. More specifically, the media through American gatekeepers created and expanded the agenda of the dominant groups and suppressed subordinate groups (Tuchman, 1978; Fishman, 1980; Megwa 1989).

The political coverage and images of Campaign '90 between Harvey Gantt and Jesse Helms were shaped by the news room staff and editors in terms of voter political reality (Shaw and McCombs, 1972). This study is an examination of the *News and Observer's* and the *Charlotte Observer's* coverage of the 1990 North Carolina Senate campaign between Harvey Gantt and Senator Jesse Helms.

Chapter one will examine the power and influence of the media from a historical perspective of the agenda-setting function of the press and the origins of Black politics in the United States.

Chapter two will consist of a review of literature of the twentieth century Negro relative to North Carolina's politics, scholars' implications of violence, and the issue of race in political campaigns and in America's political infrastructure.

Chapter three will consist of content analysis methodology employed from May through November to study the *News and*

Observer and the *Charlotte Observer* coverage of the 1990 United States Senate race between Harvey Gantt and Senator Jesse Helms.

Chapter four will consist of the results of the content analysis methodology study of the 1990 Gantt-Helms political race.

Chapter five will consist of the conclusion for this study. Thus, it will include recommendations for future studies relative to African American candidates in Southern political races.

Chapter Two

Review of Literature

The South Black Belt:
Origin of African American Political Development 1863-1877

"Power concedes nothing without a demand.
It never did, and it never will."

Frederick Douglass--1857

The concept of freedom gave Blacks impetus to withdraw from religious and social institutions controlled by whites and to chart their own economic independence within the "polity." Thus, freedom for Blacks meant being a part of the political institutions, and mobilization efforts were evident. In 1865, Blacks organized mass meetings, parades, and petitions for civil equality and the right to vote, as a result of the Emancipation.

The largest political mobilization was in areas that the Union troops had occupied during the War. In fact, Black political activity had begun before 1865 as Union leagues, Freedmen's Bureau Agents, Black soldiers and local freedmen emerged in South Carolina and Georgia to demand the right to vote and to repeal discrimination laws against Blacks. Moreover, the participation of churches and fraternal societies was vital in the Black political mobilization process. For instance, in Wilmington, North Carolina, the Freedmen's Bureau started an Equal Rights League which demanded all the social and political rights that white citizens were given. The Equal Rights League also requested that Blacks be consulted in the selection of policemen, justices of the peace, and county commissioners. In Virginia, Blacks formed secret radical political associations. For example, Richmond Blacks protested the Army's treatment of vagrants for plantation labor and later expanded their demands regarding voting and eradicating the "Rebel-controlled" local government. Like Richmond, Norfolk was occupied by Union troops in 1862. And in 1865, Blacks started the Union Monitor Club to demand equality and attempted to vote during the May election. Further, a mass meeting supported a statement written by former fugitive slave, Thomas Bayne. . . "Traitors shall not dictate or prescribe to us the terms or conditions of our citizenships" (Foner, 1970, p. 111).

Consonant with Virginia, Louisiana's mobilization process of the Black political agenda had advanced the most during the War. The support of New Orleans Tribune and radical allies continued to diffuse the issue of Blacks' right to vote. During a convention in 1865, northern white radicals, such as Governor Henry C. Warmoth and prominent "free" Black elites cast their votes to join the national Republican Party. They further requested that Congress grant Louisiana territorial rights and demanded full legal status and equality for Blacks. Of equal importance, Black mobilization efforts penetrated the sugar county, and laborers left work to attend political gatherings.

In November, the Republican Party had a "voluntary election" that attracted 20,000 voters--mostly Blacks in New Orleans--who elected Warmoth to Congress. Hence, statewide conventions in the South during 1865 and 1866 gave visibility to Black political leadership. A noted leader from North Carolina, James H. Harris, aptly stated:

> Some bring credentials, others had as much as they could do to bring themselves, having to escape from their homes stealthily at night to avoid white reprisal. (Foner, 1970, p. 112).

Also, the dedication and status of free Black ministers, artisans, and former soldiers set precedence for Black politics during Reconstruction, leading to the emergence of prominent officeholders, such as Alabama Congressman James T. Rapier and Mississippi Secretary of State, James D. Lynch. Perhaps, the most important representatives praised for their character was stated by Alexander K. McClure:

> Mississippi is exceptionable also in reputable character of her most prominent colored leaders. In all the other Southern States the Negro leaders have rivaled the white adventurers in reckless and bewildering robbery, but they have not done so in Mississippi. Three Black men have reached national fame as leaders of their race and they are all esteemed as honest men. These three men...have maintained the manhood that should be the pride of every race, and in as much as Mississippi has suffered from the carpet bag and colored rule, there has not been a tithe of demoralization and waste here that has dishonored the reign of the Black man in the Carolinas and Gulf States. That much of their comparatively good record of a bad domination is due to Revels, Bruce, and Lynch, who successfully breasted the wave of corruption, and is a fact

that should be confessed and justly appreciated (Wharton 1947, p. 212).

Hiram Rhodes Revels' was the first Negro to serve in the United States Senate, in which he served in the unexpired term of Senator Jefferson Davis. Another important figure was Blance Kelso Bruce, who was the only Negro to serve a full term in the United States Senate. Bruce was described by his colleagues as an astute political leader of the Negro race. Of equal importance was John R. Lynch, the youngest member to enter Congress, who was elected speaker in 1872 (Wharton 1947, pp. 212-216).

Moreover, the Black political mobilization had taken on new dimensions. The Governor, Henry C. Warmoth, and prominent "free" Black elites cast their votes to join the National Republican Party. They further requested that Congress grant Louisiana territorial rights and demanded full legal status and equality for Blacks. Of equal importance, Black mobilization efforts penetrated more rapidly in cities and rural areas settled by federal troops than in most of the plantation counties occupied by former slaves. Thus, the free Blacks of South Carolina and Louisiana who were responsible for Black political development remained in authority throughout Reconstruction. However, freed men from the Black belt (former slaves) would often supersede those "free" Blacks before the War.

Nevertheless, the early political conventions proved to be a valuable measure for the mobilization of Black politics. In fact, Tennessee delegates were serious toward improving their constituents' education. These delegates returned home and implemented programs that promoted Black education, protested civil officials about violent acts toward Negroes and fully demanded equality through the courts. In Georgia the Equal Rights and Educational Association established at the 1866 convention, a mandate to erect schools for Blacks to learn their rights. The program spread into fifty counties and attracted 2,000 freedmen to the political issues.

24

More striking, however, was that the new Negro leadership was no longer in its infancy. Former slaves assumed positions of prominence which were monopolized by "free Blacks" a year earlier. For instance, in Greene County, North Carolina the county's representation doubled and leaders chastised whites for violent acts toward freedmen injustices in the Labor Markets and opposition to Black education. Hence, North Carolina delegations demanded equal suffrage. A correspondent of the New Orleans Tribune in September 1866 aptly wrote, "The Negro today is not the same as he was six years ago...He has been told of his rights, which have long been robbed." "Only in 1867 would Blacks enter the 'political nation', in terms of organization, leadership, and ideology that drew upon America's Republican heritage to demand an equal place as citizens; the seeds that flowered them were planted in the first years of freedom" (Foner, 1970, p. 118).

The Twentieth Century African-American: Violence, Scholars and Mainstream Press Denigration of African-Americans

The toxins of racism and violence grew throughout America around the turn of the Twentieth Century. However, the Black community banned together religiously, socially, and politically to offset the wave of racism by whites in general, and scholars and the press in particular. The South was a cradle of the Confederacy and racism after the Civil War. Thus, Thomas Woodrow Wilson, the first Southern-born president, was sworn in, and racism became almost an official policy of the United States. Moreover, "fifty years after Appomattax, a Black man in America had reason to lament his ever having been freed, for by 1915 he was despised and ridiculed as he had never been in slavery" (Kluger, 1976, p. 85 and Foner 1970, p. 199).

25

C. Vann Woodward noted that white hatred was interwoven with the severe economic conditions in the South. Woodward further noted "permissions to hate" had been approved by people and institutions at the Apex of the American Society. The Republican Party, which supported the ideology that all men were free, changed at the close of the nineteenth century. As a result of the Spanish-American War, America noticed eight million colored people in the Caribbean and Pacific. These eight million colored people and free slaves were a political threat to the notion of white supremacy (Kluger, 1976, p. 85).

In terms of violence against Blacks in America, areas in Louisiana and Texas reached staggering proportions. In 1865 in Louisiana, Henry Adams, a North Carolinian, saw white men beating Black men as if slavery never ended. He further reported that "they govern...by the pistol and the rifle and claimed that" over two-thousand colored people" were brutally killed in Shreveport, Louisiana (Foner 1970, p. 119). Of equal importance, Texas was a state where Blacks were frequently beaten and shot like wild animals. For instance, Susan Merritt, a freedwoman, who lived in Rusk County, Texas, reported that Black bodies were floating down the Sabine River, and stated about whites: "There sure are going to be lots of souls crying against them in judgement" (Foner 1970, p. 119). In addition, whites in Pine Bluff, Arkansas, burned a Black settlement and captured its inhabitants. The whites then hung twenty-four Negro men, women, and children from the surrounding cabins. The race hatred and violence so permeated in Georgia that freedman James Jeter was beaten by whites for claiming the right to beat his own son. (Foner 1970, p. 119).

The Freedmen's Bureau agents observed that Southern whites became indignant if Blacks were treated with the same rights that they were accustomed to under slavery. An example was a North Carolina planter who complained bitterly to Union officers that a Black soldier had "bowed to me and said good morning," insisting "Blacks must never address whites unless spoken to first" (Foner 1970,

p. 119). The injustice continued in Alabama where an overseer shot a Black worker without provocation; a South Carolina minister shot a freedman through the heart when he did not expel a particular Black man from church. More astonishingly, a Black Virginian (Veteran) was beaten by whites for stating that he was proud to have served in the Union Army (Foner 1970, p. 121).

In the face of this racism and violence, white scholars, politicians, local leaders, and the press joined the white racist's dehumanization process of Negroes and remained silent or endorsed such acts. For instance, John Wesley North, a Northerner, went to Knoxville and witnessed a white mob beating a freedman. North intervened, and the mob dispersed, shocked that any person would demonstrate such an act. Later, a local white banker offered the Yankee the following advice: never in this country...interfere in behalf of a nigger" (Foner 1970, p. 121). Lastly, in 1911, in Linermore, Kentucky, a Negro was charged with murdering a white man. The Negro was captured and the most barbaric lynching of the era took place. Whites brought the Negro to the local theater and invited an audience to witness the event and empty their revolvers into the Negro's body. Thus, the lynching and violence took place, as such sadism and blatant racism often went unimpeded in the South (Kluger 1976, p. 89).

Consonant with this imperialistic racism, the press served as a conduit for the reinforcement and diffusion of white superiority. In fact, the press agents saw injustice and came around the pyre with hostility and destruction in their minds toward Blacks. The nation, for instance, viewed America's Blacks as "A varied assortment of inferior races" who were not supposed to cast their ballot." *Atlantic Monthly's* editor vividly displayed his analogy and aptly stated, "If the stronger and cleverer race is free to impose its will upon 'new-caught, sullen peoples on the other side of the globe'.... why not in South Carolina and Mississippi?" During the spring of 1900, the *New York Times* stated that denigration of the Negro's rights had saturated the nation: "Northern men...no longer denounced the suppression of the Negro vote as it used to be denounced in the Reconstruction days. The necessity of it under the supreme law of self-preservation is candidly recognized" (Kluger, 1976, p. 84-85). The vilification of the Negro as subhuman, therefore, was evident in the press. Race, then, was an issue and newspapers ("paper lynching") were the culprits. Moreover, the *Saturday Evening Post* invited racist novelist, Thomas Dixon, to describe the Negro. Dixon was successful with *The Clansman: An Historical Romance of the Ku Klux Klan*, published in 1905 and gave impetus for a racist film entitled *The Birth of a Nation*. Dixon depicted Negro characters as clowns and rapists. More strikingly, Dixon labeled Black characters as "Lady Adelia Chimpanzee and the ever popular Abraham Lincum. Lyrics about Blacks were even more horrendous. Dixon's titles included "If the Man in the Moon Were a Coon," "Go Way Back and Sit Down," "All Coons Look Alike to Me" (subtitled: "A Darkey Misunderstanding"), and "By the Watermelon Vine, Lindy Lou" (Kluger 1976, p. 84-85).

From a scholastic perspective, the press' influence on the popular culture permeated the academic community. Some of the nation's scholars at Harvard's Lawrence Scientific School (1884) cited the Negro with animalistic traits and his uncontrollable immoral behavior as logic for disenfranchisement of the entire race. In 1896, the Prudential Life Insurance Company in collaboration with the American Economics Association published a report that cited the Negro's "race traits and tendencies" were responsible for his high incidence of tuberculosis, syphilis, scrofula, and other diseases" that were said to be scientifically provable. In fact, the report further noted that the diseases were social in nature; thus the root of the problem was caused by the Black man's immorality. The philosophy of the Black man's inferiority continued to be examined by Charles Carroll's "The Negro a Beast" or "Image of God" during the 1900's. A scholar named Paul B. Barringer, chairman of the faculty at the University of Virginia, lectured the Southern Education Association in Richmond that the Negro's learning ought to be limited to a Sunday-school training." Barringer also noted that the Negro's function in life was as an incomparable "source of cheap labor for a warm climate; everywhere else he is foreordained failure, and as he knows this, he despises his own color" (Kluger 1976, p. 85).

The bitterness of racism with assistance from press agents continued to penetrate the South and made more inroads into certain scholars in the North. A clear example is Columbia University, one of the forerunners in sociology and cultural anthropology. Scholar Franklin Henry Giddings examined racist ideology as "consciousness of kind" in his principles of sociology. Giddings' colleague, William H. Dunning, viewed the enfranchisement of freedmen as "reckless... species of statecraft. Perhaps, the most damaging and intellectually shocking was from Yale's scholar William Graham Sumner "whose studies in political science and sociology blended scholarship with polemics." In 1907, Sumner's book, _Folkways_, received high praise from Southerners; other works by Sumner revealed that the Negro was backward and to improve the Negro was futile. Sumner further posited that "stateways cannot change folkways," and that the Recon-struction legislation had been vain and foolish attempts to sway the white Southerners from their beliefs; folkways were "uniform, universal in the group, imperative and invariable." "It was all foreor-dained, and though a man may curse his fate because he is born of an inferior race, his "imprecations" will go unanswered" (Kluger 1976, p. 86-87).

Another scholar named Ulrich Bonnell Phillip, in *American Negro Slavery*, had a profound effect on recasting the slavery institution into a "therapeutic practice", "a blessing to a race of backward man children (Kluger 1976, p. 86). In other words, the Negro race was viewed as a second class citizen. Ironically, a number of famous scholars and politicians from the North and South did not voice their dissention. More importantly, the Supreme Court refused to recognize Negro rights, and racism spread and continued to swell throughout the South, in particular, and America, in general. Thus, dehumanization of the Negro was the law of the land and the press continued its onslaught. *The Richmond Times* printed that "rigid segregation be applied in every relation of Southern life" (Kluger 1976, p. 86). In

Charleston, South Carolina, *"The News and Courier,* oldest newspaper in the South, opposed racial separation during 1898." *The News and Courier* further noted that such separation would prompt a "Jim Crow Bible for Colored Witnesses to Kiss" (Klugler 1976, p. 86). However, in 1906, *The News and Courier* had to digress from its position in terms of racial segregation. In fact, *The News and Observer* printed that "Segregation of the races was the only radical solution of the Negro problem in this country" (Klugler 1976, p. 86). Henceforth, the separation of races by laws and mainstream press denigration of Negroes etched a part of America's cruel history. Thus, the following legal brief aptly stated the feelings of courts:

If the progress, advancement and civilization of the twentieth century was to go forward, then it must be left, not only to the unadulterated blood of the Anglo-Saxon-Caucasian race, but to the highest types and geniuses of that race (Kluger 1976, p. 87).

The History of Race As An Issue for North Carolina Democrats and Republican Inclusion and Exclusion of Aspiring Black Politicians

Historically, the emergence of Black political leadership power was evident during the mid-Seventeenth century and after the end of the Civil War in North Carolina. Most Black Carolinians were slaves; however, some were free. Thus, the slaves and the free slaves were still faced with racial discrimination by the political system and mainstream press. In spite of those barriers, Blacks during the Emancipation era voted, held county, state, federal offices, cultivated their land, built schools, started churches, and established businesses. For instance, ten Blacks held prominent offices (state legislators in which some change developed). Upon further analysis, Negro office holders existed from 1895 through 1899. Of the ten Negro legislators, James Young, J.Y. Eaton, T.O. Fuller, and W.L. Person were college graduates. Other legislators had some formal training, such as Issac

Smith, William Crews, John T. Howe, J.H. Wright, W.C. Coates, and W.B. Henderson. Moreover, Black leadership included other federal officers, U.S. Representatives, humanitarians and educators, such as Negro Dick, Henry Evans, John Chavis, George M. Horton, James W. Hood, Warren C. Coleman, George H. White, Joseph C. Price, Henry P. Cheatham, Charles N. Hunter, Anna H. Cooper, Annie W. Holland, Charles C. Spaulding, Charlotte H. Brown, and John Dancy (Barfield, 1975, p. 1 and Edmonds, 1951, p. 97-112).

Nevertheless, the issue of race during the late 1800's to 1900's, both in terms of the political system and press coverage, caused a disenfranchisement of Negro office holders within the system. In other words, the Jim Crow laws and anti-Negro violence were major problems in North Carolina and America. Moseley (1989) asserted that "Black political power in America" was a clear reflection of the continuing social, economic, and political changes which were a vital part of the Black community's struggle for equality. Walton (1972) further posited that "no matter what the dimensions, the nature, or variety, Black politics in the final analysis reflected the Black experience in America (Moseley, 1989, p. 1 and Walton, 1977, p. 1).

Consonant with the North Carolina's political structure (establishment) of race as an issue, the misrepresentation of Blacks in general, and political leaders in particular, by the Democratic press, was vividly illustrated during the Wilmington Race Riot of 1898. Edmonds (1951) stated that printed stories during the late 1800's revealed that Negroes were in the majority and had power. Edmonds further noted that journalists wrote stories which indicated that Fusionists permitted Negroes to hold office; gave Negro police the rights to arrest whites; willfully turned the city over to Negro rule; and forced upon Wilmington social equality between the races. Moreover, news institutions represented by journalists printed stories that Wilmington was unable to meet financial obligations because of lavish spending and corrupted politics. Additionally, the white Democratic establishment and press printed that they were insulted

31

by aggressive and insolent Negroes and cohorts. Hence, they were not going to be ruled by such race.

In terms of the white Democratic establishment, the press printed viewpoints as follows:

> Negroes were given preference in the matter of employment for most of the town's artisans were Negroes, and numerous white families in the city faced bitter wants because their providers could get but little work as brick masons, carpenters, mechanics; and this economic condition was aggravated considerably by the influx of many Negroes; and Wilmington was really becoming a mecca for Negroes and a city of lost opportunities for the working class whites (Edmonds, 1951, p. 163).

Consequently, the Wilmington race issue reached a pinnacle when Alex Manly, Negro editor of *The Record and Sentinel*, responded to an editorial by a prominent Georgia white woman, who demanded the lives of Negro rapists. Manly's article was reprinted for larger circulation by Josephus Daniels, editor and Norman E. Jennett, of *The News and Observer,* a publication that had a campaign of prejudice and misrepresentation of Negro office holders. Manly's article stated thusly:

> We suggest that the whites guard their women more closely, as Mrs. Felton says, thus giving no opportunity for the human fiend, be he white or Black. You leave your goods out of doors and then complain because they are taken away. Poor white men are careless in the matter of protecting their women, especially on the farms. They are careless of their conduct toward them and our experience among poor white people in the Country teaches us that the women of that race are not any more particular in the matter of clandestine meetings with colored men than white men with colored women. Meetings of this

kind go on for some time until the woman's infatuation or the man's boldness brings attention to them and the man is lynched for rape. Every negro lynched is called 'a Big Burly Black Brute' when in fact many of these who have been thus dealt with had white men for their fathers and were not only 'not Black and burly' but were sufficiently attractive for white girls of culture and refinement to fall in love with them as is well known to all (Edmonds, 1951, p. 147).

In addition, the influence of the Democratic press on voters was heightened by Norman E. Jennett, former cartoonist. Josephus Daniels, editor of *The News and Observer* produced even more propaganda about Negro domination. In fact, *The News and Observer* headlines consisted of bitterness, vilification, misrepresentation, and prejudice to influence whites against Negroes. For instance, *The News and Observer* displayed the following headlines (Aug, 2 - no. 18): "Negro control in Wilmington", "Unbridled Lawlessness on the Streets", "Greenville Negorizied", "The Negro in Power in New Hanover", "Flagman Caught Negro Convict", "Tried to Register An Idiot", "Chicken Under His Arm," "Black Radical Convention Wants to Send Delegate to Congress," "Arrested By a Negro: He was Making No Resistance," "A Negro Insulted the Post Mistress Because He Did Not Get A Letter," "Negroism in Lenoir County," Negro on Train with Big Feet Behind White," "Negroes Have Social Equality", "Is a Race Clash Unavoidable?" Moreover, the editor of *The News and Observer* wrote that it was necessary to save Wilmington from degradation.

The Charlotte Observer headlined that the situation in Wilmington had reached an intolerable level and regretted the violence. Another newspaper, *The Wilmington Messenger* supported the heroic efforts of white liberation from Black tyranny (Edmonds, 1951, p. 141).

To further inflame the racial tension in North Carolina; Frank Weldon wrote an editorial that stated the following:

It is no secret that colored leaders, ambitious for their race, have matured in their minds a plan by which they hope to obtain absolute control of (North Carolina's) legislative, executive, and judicial machinery, and then to rapidly carry out a scheme of Canonization by which this will become a thoroughly Negro sovereign State, with that population in the majority and furnishing all officials in the public service, from U.S. Senators and Governors down through judges, legislators, and solicitors, to the last constable and janitor. If their plans succeed, North Carolina is to be the refuge of their people in America. Their brethren from all the Southern States will be invited to come here, cast their lot among their fellows, and altogether to work out their destiny in whatsoever degree of prosperity and advancement they may be able to achieve for themselves (Edmonds, 1951, p. 148).

However, a Republican newspaper, *The Union Republican*, asked more provocative questions about the Democratic press propaganda ploy. *The Union Republican* stated the following:

The Manly article was written several months before the election and before the campaign propaganda began. Why was it not right and proper to expel Manly when the article appeared? If the Democrats (press) had been sincere, Manly and his press would have been ejected long before November 11. If the riot was aimed only at Manly, what were the reasons in driving white officials out of the city and leaders (Black) of the Republican Party (Edmonds, 1951, p. 171).

Thereafter, evidence indicated that Manly did not write the letter, but the letter was written by William L. Jeffries, a white editor of *The Record*. He reprinted the article and mailed it to *The News and Observer* to engender hatred for Manly and in particular, the Black race. Ironically, Jeffries helped Manly escape from Wilmington to avoid the death mob. Of equal importance, other prominent Negroes were forced out of Wilmington, namely Tom Miller, Aaron Bryant, the Reverend I.J. Bell, Atty. Armond W. Scott, R.S. Pickens, John Dancy, John Taylor, the Manly brothers, McLain Laughton, Carter Peamon, and Issac Loften. Hence, the Wilmington race riot aided by the newspapers (press) left a profound effect on the city, the state and the South. In fact, the riot brought resentment and the migration of Blacks to other states. For the Negroes left in Wilmington, Black participation in the political process and respect for the system was doomed (Edmonds, 1951, pp. 158-174).

Undoubtedly, the mainstream newspapers in the South during the late 1800's exerted powerful influence on race issue campaigns. In fact, *The News and Observer* partisanship with the political system was cruel in its coverage of Blacks, in general, and political leaders, in particular. The editors later observed that The News and Observer's depiction of Blacks was vindictive. Equally important, the editors noted that stories about Blacks were not winnowed before publication. As Edmonds (1951) noted, Black news stories were in full bloom for manipulative purposes.

Thus, many whites voted a racial ticket in 1898 in concert with *The News and Observer's* depiction of races. Blacks suffered the repercussion for political aspirants in general and office holders in particular. As a matter of fact, the relationship between the Democratic Party and press diluted Black political leadership.

By the 1900's, the issue of Negro race domination was evident in Democrats, Fusionists, Republicans and the press. For Blacks, in general, all parties to a great extent were in collaboration to enact laws to prohibit Negroes from full participation in the political arena. Moreover, if not in complete agreement, vicious accusations were launched toward any party who supported Negro domination in the mainstream press, namely by *The News and Observer* (Edmonds, 1951 and Luebke 1990).

Specifically, then, Josephus Daniels, editor, was sent to Louisiana for reportage of disfranchisement amendments. Thus, Daniels reported that Louisiana's plan of suffrage "placed politics on a new level." In fact, Daniels further noted that the Populists caused a return to the Democratic Party as a result of attempts to free white women from Negroes' domination and to exclude ignorant Negroes from political office and to insure that white men, illiterate or otherwise, obtained a ballot. Daniel's news story was used by Democratic politicians who influenced the entire political structure in North Carolina. The Democratic Party and press coverage which connected Populists and Republicans as Negro-lovers signaled a powerful message to readers. For that matter Populists and Republicans collaborated to achieve their political agendas. Moreover, the Republican Party substantiated their disloyalty to the Negro race after the election of 1900. A noted Republican, Jeter C. Pritchard, won his 1894-1896 with Negro votes. However, in 1902, Pritchard stated that Republicans were not concerned with the Negro party. Thus, the Republican Party became "lily white." Conversely, Johnson, a Populist from Sampson County, echoed his party sentiments and stated that "the Negroes, they ought never to have been given the right of suffrage when they were." Johnson further declared "that white people should and would rule." Thus, Negroes in general, and Negro office holders in particular, were not considered part of the political system. Simply stated, each party's platform regarding the Negro's legitimacy to vote or hold office was questioned. Further, each party saw the Negro race as a major issue which caused fear among White people.

The Democratic Party's partnership with the mainstream press in depiction and racial misrepresentation of Negro office holders had a profound effect across the state. Consequently, the powerful impact of the press' news stories of Negro race denomination printed by news organizations rendered control to the Democratic Party during the dawn of the Twentieth Century. The Democratic propaganda machine prevailed in the overthrow of the Fusionists, the Wilmington race riot, the disfranchisement amendment, and using the judicial process to their advantage. The Democratic Party and press influences were evident in the exclusion of Negroes' political participation for at least fifty years (Edmonds, 1951, pp. 220-222 and Luebke, 1990).

African-American Tarheel Politics and Civil Rights Movements' Political Impact

In V.O. Key's classic book (1949), *Southern Politics*, North Carolina was viewed as a progressive plutocracy under Democratic domination. This progressive image or myth was not the reality of North Carolina's political establishment. The issue of race was still a political instrument to be used toward facilitating the Negro's upward mobility by the two-party system. Clearly, Key also acknowledged that the race issue was suppressed in North Carolina for fifty years through a political process in which political leaders operated their election campaign within the accepted framework" and an "unspoken" code that failed to arouse racial tension. The Negro then was paternalistic (Bass et al. 1977).

An astute chief political writer for *The News and Observer*, Ferrel Guillory, stated that "the further you get from North Carolina, the more progressive it looks." However, the reality of race and press coverage of political appeals on race within campaigns was a powerful force to be reckoned with. The president of the University of North Carolina at Chapel Hill, Frank Porter Graham, who campaigned for a full term for the U.S. Senate proved this fact. Key (1949) viewed Graham as "the South's most "prominent educator and versatile public servant" who represented American progressivism." In fact, Graham did not smoke, drink, or use profanity. These were fashionable characteristics for the traditional conservative state. In the primary of the senate election, Graham won a 49.1 percentage of votes against Willis Smith, former president of the American Bar Association and Chairman of Duke University's Board. Hence,

Smith called for a run-off which followed the race-baiting campaign in Florida of liberal Senator Claude Pepper and George Smathers, a declared racist. Of equal importance, the U.S. Supreme court had ruled the integration of Pullman dining cars and the University of Texas and Oklahoma admittance of Negro' students. Graham and his campaign followers were completely confident. However, during the end of the election, literature and press coverage flooded the state. The power of the media institutions' headlines was evident. Press news headlines declared "Frank Graham Favors Mingling of the Races", "Wake Up, White People Before It is Too Late", "End of Racial Segregation Proposed," "The South Under Attack," and "Do You Know that 28 Percent of the North Carolina Population is Colored?" The notion was that Frank Graham was an integrationist and would end racial segregation (Luebke 1990, p. 17).

Moreover, there were handbills distributed throughout the state which pictured a Negro' youth whom Graham appointed to West Point. As a matter of fact, the Negro' had been placed at West Point but in an alternate status. Writer, Samuel Lubell, reported that Graham took a white youth who was accepted at West Point to a tobacco-farming community to discredit Willis' racial propaganda campaign. Lubell further asserted that after Graham's speech a vicious racial question lurked through the crowd: "Why didn't he bring the nigger he appointed? Who is he trying to fool, showing us that white boy?" (Bass and DeVries 1977, p. 220).

In addition, the power of the press coverage of racial appeals transcended the economic industry as well as some white elites. Lubell's interview in a suburban area in Greensboro revealed that whites were in support of Eisenhower Republicans (1952) but respected Graham's progressive reputation as an educator. Lubell aptly stated:

> One worker for Willis Smith had written an eloquent campaign letter, picturing the threat to family security in

inflationary policies which robbed siblings of their value and which taxed away so much of one's earnings. She showed the letter to the wife of a doctor, who campaigned for Graham in the first primary. The doctor's wife read it and exclaimed. "That's a fine letter! It expresses my sentiments exactly." Then, as she turned to leave, the doctor's wife added "You know I don't want my daughter to go to school with negroes."(Bass and DeVries 1977, p. 220).

The United States senate race yielded Willis Smith as the winner of eighteen eastern counties which Graham won in the primary race. These counties were heavily populated with Blacks and Smith's racial appeal coverage by the press affected Graham's political aspirations. Lubell concluded with these assertions:

> The surprise in Graham's defeat was the revelation that the cry of 'Nigger' could inflame even the well-educated, well-to-do middle class...It was not only the bigots who turned against 'Doctor Frank' but many "progressive North Carolinians" (Bass and DeVries 1977, p. 221).

In a precinct analysis, Lubell reported that voting patterns for Smith's election in North Carolina paralleled to Smather's race-baiting campaign in Florida in which Dixiecrates and Republicans were key supporters for presidential candidates in 1948. In other words, Lubell's analysis substantiated the emergence of economically and racially staunch voters who formed the foundation for the New Republican Party in North Carolina and the South. Later, Graham asserted that Smith's campaign and the way press coverage depicted him as a monster caused communication problems amongst his friends (Bass and DeVries, p. 221).

Since the Graham and Smith senate race, the issue of race and press coverage manifested and emerged in other political elections covertly or overtly. For instance, in 1956, North Carolina

Congressman Thurmond Chatman and Charles B. Deave lost their election because they failed to sign the "Southern Manifesto" that denounced the Supreme Court's school desegregation decisions, although Congressman, Harold Cooley, who refused to sign, won his election. In addition, congressional delegation's voting record toward Negroes was Conservative during this era. *The Congressional Quarterly* reported that from 1965-74 North Carolina ranked behind Mississippi on civil rights legislation. Further, Dr. T. Beverly Lake's campaign (1960's) was an example of racial tactics and further demonstrated that the "progressive" image was a myth. In 1972, the racial issue climaxed the Jesse Helms Republican Campaign. Helms, the first state (Republican) senator in the Century, was an conservative and crusaded against busing, civil rights legislation, and the civil rights movement (Bass and DeVries, pp. 221-222). More importantly, Helms, as an experienced professional in the media as a writer, commentator, and editorialist, understood the media impact in political campaigns. Further, Helms used race and media as an instrument to stifle Negroes' "political" progression, either overtly or covertly (Bass and DeVries, pp. 221-222).

However, the significant impact of the U.S. Supreme Court's 1954 decision, Brown vs. Topeka Board of Education, and major media coverage of the Civil Rights movement, thrust forth new Black leaders in the political arena in general and Tarheel Politics in particular. The sentiments toward Blacks' social and political rights were still not accepted by some "movers and shakers".

The progressive ideology or image then that North Carolina's political leaders espoused, such as governors, business leaders, and press was tested even more in the 50's and 60's. These progressive leaders and media institutions, including current Governor Luther Hodges, felt that the U.S. Supreme Court was wrong in ruling school desegregation. Hence, Governor Luther Hodges introduced the Pearsall plan to maintain the segregated status quo. The Pearsall plan gave educational grants to parents who wanted to send their children to private schools in avoidance of desegregation. Of utmost importance, most mainstream newspaper institutions supported the Pearsall plan. The newspaper institutions felt that Governor Hodges was morally right in his attempt to achieve racial harmony. *The Fayetteville Observer* headline was "A Fire Extinguisher." *The Greensboro Daily News* stated that the "Tortuous and narrow path ahead," indicated that the Pearsall plan aided North Carolina to tread it safely. The Washington Post called busing "the country's most volatile domestic political issue." However, the Pearsall plan failed, and North Carolina saw national press coverage of the Civil Rights movement, and Tarheel politics change its racial composition. Hence, there was major unrest in North Carolina, unrest was deeply rooted in racial concern and political leaders sharing power (Powell 1989, pp. 517-529).

On February 1, 1960, four students, David Richmond, Franklin McCain, Ezell Blair, Jr., and Joseph McNeil, college students from North Carolina A&T State University tested the desegregation landmark decision in Brown vs. Board of Education. The four students went downtown to Woolworth's, sat down and ordered a cup of coffee. They were not served but stayed until the store closed. They returned the next day and were later joined by other students who occupied sixty-three of the sixty-five seats at Woolworth's. Hence, there were crowds of supporters, white hecklers, newspapers, radios, and television reporters which included national networks and news magazines. The situation spread to other parts of North Carolina, such as Winston-Salem, Durham, Chapel Hill, Charlotte, and Raleigh. The Civil Rights movement now involved school integration and sit-ins which proved to thrust the Blacks in North Carolina into a new era, both socially and politically (Luebke 1990, pp. 102-105).

More importantly, the passage of the Civil Rights Act of 1964 and the Voting Act of 1965 set new dynamics in North Carolina; however, racial resistance resurfaced in Wilmington in 1971. Ben Chavis, a United Church of Christ minister and member of the UCCC's Commission for social justice , visited Wilmington, to help settle a court order for school desegregation, resulting in whites'

41

resistance in the city. Chavis began to work with high school students to settle differences with the all-white school board. The negotiations were fruitless and violence occurred. Later, Chavis noted that power meticulously utilized could be a powerful political tool for Blacks. Bennett (1968) noted that the Black protest continued to gain momentum as Blacks won concession. Bennett also noted that Blacks' apathy and despair had dissipated. The Civil Rights movement gave Blacks new vision for democracy. Rustin (1965) noted that the Black participation in protest marches, boycotts and urban rebellions were processors that Blacks effectively utilized to gain entrance into the Twentieth Century political establishment (Moseley 1989, pp. 3-7).

Verba and Nie (1972) aptly stated the following with regard to the Black race:

> If there is any impact on participation associated more directly with race, it is one that gives some boost to Black citizens, particularly if they have a sense of group consciousness. Black Americans have in group consciousness a great resource of political development (Moseley 1989, p. 6).

Nelson and Merants asserted the success of electorate officials:

> Civil rights action on the national level was, of course, an important stimulant in this process, but local civil rights activities were even more significant.

Numerous demonstrations and other activities performed the double function of involving in direct political action thousands of Blacks who had previously been politically inactive and at the same time exposed the stubborn racism of the white establishment. The combination of these factors contributed to several developments: It encouraged a growing number of Blacks to engage in politics; it shattered the notion that Blacks were experiencing normal progress and thus were satisfied with their lot; it reinforced the idea that Blacks had to act in unison, not as individuals, if they wanted to improve their socio-economic-political conditions, and it provided Blacks with a growing sense of group consciousness and cohesion" (Moseley 1989, p. 4).

African-American Tarheel's State and Federal Candidates Since Reconstruction

The participation of Blacks in the political establishment since Reconstruction was a direct result of the civil rights movement. As noted historian, H.G. Jones, pointed out, "These victories reflected more than a growing Black vote; they also reflected the willingness of some whites to vote for minority candidates." Jones further asserted that Blacks constituted 22 percent of the population in North Carolina; yet, Blacks held only 255 or 5 percent of its 5,037 elective offices.

In 1968, Reginald A. Hawkins, a Charlotte dentist, was the first Black who made a bid for a statewide office. Hawkins ran for governor and received in the Democratic primary 129,808 votes; however, his two white opponents, who were sons of former governors, together gained 571,292 votes. Henry E. Frye of Guilford County in Greensboro became the first Black elected to the General Assembly since Reconstruction. Frye also was the first Black on the North Carolina Supreme Court. In 1969, Howard Lee became the first Black mayor of Chapel Hill, a predominantly white southern town. Lee was also the first Black to hold a Cabinet position under the leadership of Governor James B. Hunt in 1977. In 1972, Lee ran for Congress and lost against a white opponent, incumbent L.H. Fountain. Lee garnered 41 percent of the vote and his campaign activated 18,000 Blacks in the rural areas to vote for the first time. Election analysis indicated that less than half of the registered Blacks cast their ballot. Moreover, Clarence Lighner became the mayor of Raleigh in 1973. Of equal importance, Black legislators saw the need for building cross-sectional racial support for statewide leadership. H.M. Michaux, first

43

Black state representative from Durham in 1972, ran for Attorney General in 1974; however, he lost.

Despite these victories for Black Tarheel politicians, the issue of race was subconsciously or consciously in the minds of white North Carolinians and politicians. As noted historian John Hope Franklin in his book, *The Free Negro in North Carolina 1790-1860*, spoke of Blacks as "an unwanted people," the validity of such title was evident in the race-baiting which appeared in political campaigns during the mid-70's throughout the 90's. For instance, in 1976, white tradition-alist Jimmy Green utilized newspaper ads in eastern North Carolina (heavily populated with small towns) which depicted a picture of his Black opponent, Howard Lee. Green's ad revealed that "unless the people came out to vote on September 14, the election will be decided by a relatively small segment of the population." Green's coded message was the importance of white votes in counterance of Black vote turnout. Moreover, in 1982, the Second Congressional District run-off election was between Mickey Michaux and former state legislator and congressman, Tim Valentine. Michaux won 42 percent of the vote and white traditionalist Valentine, from Nash County (heavily populated with rural voters), won 58 percent. Subsequently, Valentine distributed an anti-Michaux "Dear Neighbor" flyer among rural and urban white voters in the same context of the Graham and Smith campaign. Valentine's flyer asked voters "whether you want to be represented in Congress by a big-government, free-spending liberal with close ties to labor bosses." Valentine's message preceded with "It is not easy to stop and take time to vote, but you must. Our polls indicate that the same well organized Black vote which was so obvious and influential in the First Primary will turn out again on July 27. My opponent will again be busing his supporters to the polling places in record number." The coded race language was in the words of a "Black vote" and "busing." Hence, Michaux did not receive any more votes from Whites in comparison to the First Primary (Luebke, 1990, pp. 114-120).

Race as an Issue: Harvey Gantt's South Carolina and North Carolina Heritage and Bid for the North Carolina 1990 United States Senate Race

"Chosen is the word I'd use, He always seemed to have been marked for some special role. Everything he set out to do, he did."

Gloria Gantt

The optimism and determination that Harvey Gantt possessed were deeply rooted in his religious upbringing in the South. In 1943, Gantt was born to the proud parents, Christopher Columbus Gantt, Jr. and Wilhelmenia Gantt in a public housing project located in Charleston, South Carolina. Gantt's family had ancestors whose slaves' heritage was on the sea island rice plantations. Gantt's father was a determined man who wanted his five children to receive a better education in the segregated system. Hence, Gantt's father worked as a shipyard mechanic, carpenter, and in a dry cleaners (Ahearn, October 25, 1990). Harvey Gantt took heed to his family's work ethics and employed those same traits in his academic as well as political career. Gantt recalled that his segregated high school (Burke) had outstanding teachers who taught him Latin, Greek Mythology, and Chemistry. Gantt further noted that those teachers were positive role models. In fact, those teachers instilled the ingredients of success in a segregated system. Gantt was also inspired to challenge such a system during the civil rights era. Thus, Gantt was arrested the night teachers at Burke High School arranged a dinner to honor four graduating seniors. Gantt had participated in a nonviolent protest to integrate Kress-Five and Dime on King Street in Charleston, South Carolina. Gantt's father, supported his son's social and political endeavors (Ahearn, October 25, 1991). Moreover, Gantt continued to challenge the laws of South Carolina. Gantt's father, who was a long-time member of the (NAACP), National Association for the Advancement of Colored People, supported his son's

45

entrance in Clemson University. Gantt had left home and attended Iowa University in Ames, Iowa, for two years majoring in Architectural Design. However, Gantt saw the need to study at a university near his home town. In 1963, Gantt's entry into Clemson University was historic. Governor Ernest Hollings was responsible for orchestrating such an historic event. Governor Hollings further warned the student body of the U.S. Supreme Court's ruling in Brown vs. Board of Education and University of Mississippi riots. Harvey Gantt graduated from Clemson University and married Lucinda Brawley, the second Black student at Clemson University. Later, Harvey Gantt delved into mayoral politics which gave his name even more recognition. Gantt moved to Charlotte, North Carolina and became the first Black mayor. Gantt was viewed as a mark of race progress in the South--North Carolina.

Gantt's political astuteness was further substantiated nearly twenty-seven years later when he entered the U.S. Senate race. The race was indeed historic in a sense because no Black person had run for or won such office since the Reconstruction Era. Gantt's platform centered on the elderly, education, economy and environment, issues that every North Carolinian had to confront. Thus, his platform reached across racial lines and was of utmost importance to the future of North Carolina.

A speech by Harvey Gantt in Smithfield, North Carolina aptly stated his views:

> I believe that government has a role to play in improving the quality of life for all of us. I came from, as many of you have heard me say many times, from very humble circumstances... parents who didn't have much in the way of education, but believed in America. A lot of people can tell that story. Parents with an 8th grade education, but they never felt disadvantaged. Parents who were treated like second-class citizens, but they always felt like the promise of America could be made real in their lifetime

and for their children. We said education, environment, doing something about health care in this nation, attending to the social problems that affect us all, poverty, illiteracy, infant mortality rates, that has more to do with--more to do with making North Carolina better than worrying about funding a few artists around this country.

Gantt further noted:

America is an idea planted in all our minds that says if you believe in access, opportunity and the fact that people can move forward if they've got initiative to do so, then great things happen in this country. I want the promise of America made real to working families in this country. I want this country to turn its attention to its most important resource...the people of America. It is about whether or not we feel it's important to make our children the smartest ever. It's about whether or not you're going to deliver decent health care to our senior citizens as well as your youngest among us. It's about whether or not we're going to care about God's green earth and preserve the environment (Effrow, pp. 1-2, October 25, 1990).

Jesse Helms' North Carolina Heritage

"The small-town, Southern segregationist values of
his youth are the values he holds dear and votes for. Some of
those values are good-support for home patriotism and religion.
They also include a large quantity of racism."

Ted Arrington

Jesse Helms has been revered as a man who championed the conservative causes. Helms stands for moral issues, not for immoral ones. With that conservative agenda, the factor of race plays a key role in Jesse's upbringing. He does not see a need for government regulations on schools and social problems that stemmed directly from segregated systems which is deeply rooted in his value system. Having grown up during the Depression era in a small town, Monroe, located southeast of Charlotte, he was the son of Jesse Alexander Helms, Sr., Monroe's fire chief during the 20's and 30's. Helms, at age 69, reminisced about those segregated years. "I shall always remember the shady streets, the quiet Sundays, the cotton wagons, the Fourth of July parades." Helms further recalled the stream of school kids marching uptown to place flowers on the courthouse square monument during Confederate Memorial Day.

Critics, however, pointed to other dark realities of such a period in American history and stated that Jesse Helms' idyllic years were periods of segregation and racism. During that time Blacks stayed in segregated schools and neighborhoods; middle and upper class women did not seek careers, and mill workers rarely challenged the status quo (*Babington News Observer*, 9A, Oct. 31, 1990).

Nevertheless, Helms' childhood days were marked by success. Delivering papers, and working as a soda jerk part-time, Jesse later found a job that challenged his writing skills. He was hired to write football game coverage by the *Monroe Journal.* In 1938, Helms graduated from high school at fifteen and stated in the school yearbook that he was an aspiring columnist. Later, Helms was a student at Wingate College for a year. The following year he enrolled at Wake Forest University, taking odd jobs as a dishwasher, utility worker, and college news writer. He also worked at night for 50 cents as a proof-reader for the *News and Observer* and was later offered a full-time job. Helms declined the job and entered radio as a newsperson at a station in Roanoke Rapids, North Carolina. "The skinny kid from Monroe would soon have a voice to notice" (Babington, 9A, News and Observer, Oct. 31, 1990).

In 1948, Jesse Helms joined WRAC, a 250-watt station owned by a political conservative, A.J. Fletcher. However, by 1950 Helms left journalism to work for Willis Smith, who was running against the incumbent Frank Porter Graham, former president of The University of North Carolina in Chapel Hill. The Senate race was marked by race baiting and red baiting. In fact, Smith backers depicted a picture of Graham's wife dancing with a Black man. Thus, the literature distributed by Smith backers criticized Graham for opposing segregation. Helms denied any connection with those campaign's tactics. Willis Smith won the election, and Jesse Helms went to Washington as Smith's administrative assistant. Later, he returned to Raleigh after Senator Smith's death and worked as the executive director of the North Carolina Bankers Association. *The Tarheel Banker* was a magazine where Helms wrote personal columns reflecting his conservative views.

For instance, in 1955 Helms wrote the following: "Unless our Negro citizens submit more easily than we predict they will, North Carolina does not have the simple choice between segregated schools and integrated schools. Our only choice is between integrated public schools and free choice private schools. The decision will have been made by a very small minority of people who are hell-bent on forced integration." Helms later commented on the Little Rock, Arkansas integration process: "What is happening in America is exactly in tune with the forecasts of Karl Marx. The cackles you hear have a Russian accent" (Babington, 9A, *News and Observer*, Oct. 3, 1990).

Elected to the Raleigh City Council in 1957, Helms served two terms and voted against all increased spending proposals. However, in 1960, he returned to WRAL TV at the request of A.J. Flecher. As an editorialist he aired five minutes of commentary of racial resentment, touching upon "Great Society Programs," "Civil rights movement," "liberals," "socialized medicine," and "government spending.." Helms' daily editorials were also printed in many small newspapers. This type of notoriety gave Helms a conservative alignment of voters and sympathizers which proved to be noteworthy in 1972 (Babington, 9A, *News and Observer*, Oct. 31, 1990).

The North Carolina United States Senate Race: % Results Between Harvey Gantt and Senator Jesse Helms

The North Carolina campaign race for the United States Senate between Jesse Helms and Harvey Gantt proved to be a classic race-baiting campaign. In fact, the final weeks of the election attracted state-wide and national coverage. In this highly charged, racially motivated campaign Jesse Helms placed a number of negative ads assailing his opponent. Helms accused Gantt, the Black former mayor of Charlotte, of supporting racial quotas. More astonishingly, Helms purported that Gantt profited from the sale of a television station's stock under minority status and had a "secret campaign" with homosexuals. Of equal importance, Helms had the support of the state Republican Party 's mailing racial postcards to heavily Democratic Black precincts (Guillory, page 1A, November 7, 1990; Christensen, page 1, November 7, 1990).

Additionally, the barrage of negative ads by Jesse Helms combined with voters' machine problems, paper ballots, and judicial intervention during election night added to the white backlash. In other words, the machine problems and judicial intervention favored Helms' traditional values ideology (Riley, 1A-17A, Nov 7, 1990, Guillory 1A, Nov 7, 1990).

Guillory noted that in a poll conducted by voter research and surveys from more than 2,000 North Carolina voters had changed their minds and voted for Jesse Helms. Guillory further noted that 14% of the change was a result of potent negative ads and the presence of Jesse Helms in North Carolina final weeks after Congress adjourned. Hence, the senator told voters to view the election as being between a conservative Jesse Helms and a liberal Harvey Gantt. Helms' political ads further depicted a white worker being rejected for a job through written communication and an announcer indicating that a less qualified Black worker having received the job. This type of race baiting campaign impacted many North Carolina voters who were undecided. Equally important, Jesse Helms' campaign lured crossover "conservative Democrats - *Jessecrats*" who registered 27 percentage points. A typical Helms supporter was Leroy Goodman, who stated that Helms was one of them. Further, he stated that Helms was a winner and decried the negative campaigning. Another typical Helms' supporter was Eddie Lyons, who stated that "I voted for ol' Jesse," because of racial quotas and gays. I didn't like the minority trick, scam (Gantt's television role). "And the gay rights, queers, whatever they want to be called, I don't go for that" (Riley, p. 17A, Nov 7, 1990). The impact of Helms' ideology and ads was evident, reaching most of North Carolina's white undecided voters, in particular, and white voters, in general. In the wake of the election, then, Helms, who campaigned on traditional values and race as issues won 65 percent of the white vote and 6 percent of the Black vote. In fact, he carried most of the state, especially the eastern and coastal area of North Carolina. For the most part, these areas were heavily populated with rural whites whose traditional values Helms embodied.

Helms received strong support from white males in small towns and the countryside. The overall voting outcome registered Harvey Gantt - 463,776,339 and Jesse Helms - 893,882,543. Triumphantly Helms decried that "Cheap politicians" had made his family suffer. He further enthusiastically apologized to his supporters for being late. I've been home watching the grieving face of Dan Rather.

> There's no joy in Mudville tonight. The Mighty Ultra-liberal establishment   the liberal politicians and editors and commentators and columnists have struck out again... There has been a multitude of upturned noses in this campaign, as you and I have spoken of North Carolina values... There has been pretense that our adversaries did not understand what we were talking about... Well, maybe they now understand (Christensen, 1A, Nov. 7, 1990).

Babington noted that Helms later poked fun at the state's major newspaper who endorsed Harvey Gantt. Ironically, Helms' election to his fourth term as U.S. Senator mirrored the divisive nature of race during his political campaign which damaged North Carolina's progressive image (Babington, 15A, Nov 7, 1990).

Chapter Three

Media Effects and Agenda-Setting Functions of the Press

Agenda-setting theory posits that the news media are influential in the social processes that create reality. Scholars further posit that through a selective process embedded within the social and psychological factors construct, the media constrict the individual's perceived social reality (Tuchman, 1978, Fishman, 1980, Gandy, 1982, Lang and Lang, 1981, Grober, 1984, McCombs and Shaw, 1972). Since agenda setting and politics underscore this study, this chapter examines the agenda setting frame and powerful effects of media.

Specifically, this chapter discusses historical and political implications of African American politicians and agenda setting relative to the influences of the press in the social and political process. An emerging corpus of research indicates that powerful actors, groups, and institutions who are familiar with the symbolic strategies used by gatekeepers in determining and defining news continue to set the agenda of the news media (Weaver and Elliott, 1984; Turks, 1986; Gandy, 1982; Becker, 1982; Megwa and Brenner, 1986; Megwa, 1987, Megwa and Brenner, 1988b.)

This chapter emphasizes that the American media's selection of "news" stories is based on the values of media institutions and gatekeepers. American gatekeepers' needs and expectations in terms of "news" and "race" were embedded in American culture and values. In other words, the communication process is part of cognitive relationships and ideas specific to culture. Moreover, Schramm notes that the mass communication process in any human society is controlled by cultural and group self-interest as well as by cultural expectations. Schramm further noted that the American mass media reporting is a conduit through which individuals defined their views of the world and reinforced their values. Hence, it is too simple to assume a global village in which everyone's needs and values merge toward an American norm. The political and race conflicts between and within cultures are real and the media illuminated that image (Lewin 35 al. 1964; Schramm, 1964).

Shaw and McCombs (1972) conjecture that in political campaigns, information and images in the mass media influence voters' perception of candidates. Such information and story composition in the mass media are only variables many voters used in the decision-making process. Thus, news room staff, editors, and powerful political actors shape voter's political reality (Shaw and McCombs, 1987). The chapter concludes with a critical analysis of the political race between Harvey Gantt and Senator Jesse Helms.

A Worldly Perspective:
Theoretical Framework of the Four Theories of the Press and Its Functions Socially and Politically

The theoretical framework of the four theories of the press was conceptualized by noted scholars: Siebert, Peterson, and Schramm. These scholars believed that the press operated social and politically within any system in accordance with that system's social and political structure. Thus, the communication processes were interwoven with cognitive relative relationships to that society.

In other words, media co-existed with citizens' societal beliefs about the nature of humanity and the levels of truth and knowledge (Siebert, Peterson, Schramm, 1956).

In 1956, Siebert, Peterson, and Schramm conceptualized and proposed four theories namely: The Authoritarian, the Libertarian, the Communist, and the Social Responsibility. The Authoritarian theory asserted that citizens in an Authoritarian society had to espouse to governmental preservation of peace and order. Further, he stated that advancement of civilization had precedence over one's individual freedom. Moreover, the Authoritarian philosophy suggested that leaders' intelligence and foresight gave them dominant power to lead the state over common people. The theory further asserted that leaders were appointed by divine power. Of equal importance, leaders had apprehension about the press's influence and felt threatened. Hence, the leaders gave licenses to press owners who supported their ideology and demanded copies of stories to be re-examined by governmental officials for approval. Finally, the Authoritarian theorists supported and believed that the public did not possess the aptitude to decipher governmental problems.

The Libertarian theorists, on the other hand, proposed that individuals had the right to make decisions and to determine their destiny in society. Libertarians further maintained that society constituted diverse groups. Specifically, such theorists believed that an "open marketplace of ideas" allowed different opinions to be debated amongst its citizenry and provided a more "just" system of government. Moreover, the Libertarian theory gave the media the right to serve as watchdogs over government. Libertarian theorists then had changed individuals' attitudes toward the media. More importantly, the implications of Libertarian theory were embedded in America at the end of the Eighteenth Century and its U.S. Constitution by the Framers.

The Communist theorists believed that the government's control of media was just and that the media served as an ideological tool to indoctrinate the masses toward state goals. Additionally, if there were criticism that stemmed from the government, it was by high-ranking party officials, not the public disseminating information to the masses nor the masses themselves.

The Social Responsibility theorists during the Twentieth Century believed "that freedom carried concomitant obligations; and the press...had to be responsible to society... the public's right to know rather than publisher's right to speak" (Siebert, et. al 1956, p. 91). In other words, Social Responsibility theorists believed that the media should provide accurate, fair, complete information, not interwoven with the media's own biases, half truths, and deliberate lies (Siebert, et al. 1956).

A Conceptual Framework of Attitudes, Values and Perceptions

Attitudes

Some scholars emphasized that the conceptualization of attitudes was rooted in the tradition of the disciplines of sociologists and psychologists. Thus, explanations then regarding the formation of attitudes in human beings were explicated more clearly in terms of scientific inquiry from these researchers.

Thomas and Znaniecki (1918) theorized that the social psychology process was the scientific study of attitudes. They further noted that an individual's mental processes were a direct result of attitudes formation toward responses in the social world. Thus, a person's attitude then was his or her mental state toward a value or values that were embedded in social cultures (Thomas and Znaniecki, 1918, p. 19).

However, Thurstone (1946) defined attitudes with a broader definition in understanding human behavior. Thurstone offered this explanation:

> Attitudes were the ...intensity of positive or negative effect for or against a psychological object. Thus the term psychological object was any symbol, person, phrase, slogan or concept in which an individual viewed as positive or negative (Thurstone, 1946, p. 40).

Kretch, et. al. (1948) suggested that the formation of attitudes was firmly embedded during one's social and culture interactions. In other words, attitudes reflected the values, norms, and beliefs of the individual's group(s) (Kretch and Crutchfield, 1948, p. 102).

Sherif (1965) suggested that the developmental process of human beings and their life experiences brought them from a neutral viewpoint to opinion formation. In other words, a person's attitude referred to his stance as it relates to issues, whether personal or within groups or institutions. Sherif (1965) stated aptly in his writing:

> We speak of an individual's attitudes when we refer to his holding in high esteem his own family, his own school, his own political party, his own religion, with all the emotional and affective overtones these terms imply.... we refer to one's attitudes when we say one holds other

groups, political parties, other schools or religions in a less favorable light or at a safe distance (as "safe" was defined by his attitude formation (Sherif, 1965, p. 4).

Further, Sherif believed that when a person engaged in specific situations that his behavioral pattern was predictable. In other words, the author maintained that objects that were inconsistent with a person's behavioral pattern became undesirable. He further noted that the person's behavior patterns enabled him to decide whether or not a person's attitudinal disposition was prevalent. The inferences of attitudes, then, stemmed from predictable and characteristic modes of behavior issues, persons or events over a period of time (Sherif and Conhit, 1947; Sherif, 1948; Campbell, 1950; Hoveland, et al., 1953; Sherif and Sherif, 1956; Janis, et al., 1959.

Rokeach (1968) indicated that the definition of attitude was consonant with Kretch. Attitude then was "relatively" a part of inter-related beliefs in which cognitive, affective and behavioral components were interwoven.

Hence, Rokeach asserted that the foundation, of attitudes was interwoven with social, cultural and psychological factors. Thus, attitudes, to a degree, were firmly embedded in group(s) in which individuals were committed. Attitudes mirrored the values, norms, and beliefs of group(s).

Values

LaPiere (1934) stated that "values were observed motives, the object, quality, or condition that satisfies the motivation." Becker (1941) posited that "values were any object of any need".

According to Fromm (1947), individuals in a society were not free to make a decision to have values or not to have values. Individuals were free only to discriminate between different values. In other words, Fromm believed that values were natural or societal, and individuals were inextricably linked to a value system in society.

Dodd (1950) noted that the term "value" was something desired for or selected by a person to justify his/her behavior. Landberg (1950) stated that an object was a value if people viewed it as important to their human existence.

Znaniecki (1952) underscored the importance of understanding the social structure accessible to those members of a particular group. Thus, he believed that by understanding their social values we could understand more clearly that group. This empirical content is accessible to the members of some social group and gives meaning with regard to their activities. Jacob (1962, p. 28) acknowledged that values were "normative standards by which human beings were influenced in their choice among the alternative courses of action which they perceived."

According to Vander Zander, "values" were the criteria used in evaluating objects, events, feelings or ideas (1970, p. 57). Consonant with Vander Zander's philosophy, Kluckhohn expounded on the values concept and stated:

> A value was a conception distinctive of an individual or group which influenced the selection process. Thus, a value implied a certain code or standard (Kluger, 1976, pp. 86–87).

Rokeach defined values as a belief that a specific mode of conduct was preferable to a converse mode of conduct. More specifically, Rokeach outlined his concept relative to human values:

- the antecedents of human values were embedded in culture, society and its institutions, and personality.

- the total number of values an individual possessed was small.

59

- values were part of value systems.

- all humans possessed the same values to some degree.

- human values were manifested in all phenomena in social scientists investigation and understanding.

More succinctly, Rokeach further posited his "concept of values and opined":

The concept of values was essential across all social sciences. More profoundly, values were the important dependent variable in the study of society, personality, and culture and the most important independent variable in the study of social attitudes and behavior (Rokeach, 1973, p. 4).

Perceptions

Since the early years of 1892, the definition of perception has been defined by various theoretical concepts, in that the study of perception is a simple direct task of accumulating easily obtained and easily understood data. Hence, Allport asserted that perception was equally as important as attitude in evaluating telecommunication. Allport also viewed perception as having to do with one's awareness of one's surrounding or conditions. One's dependency depended largely upon the impressions those objects or conditions impinged on one's senses (Allport, 1955).

Koffka stated that visual perception raised the question, "Why do things look as they do?" Koffka concluded "we then interpreted perception as covering the awareness of complex instructional situations as well as single objectives" (Koffka, 1935).

Bartley noted that perception was not restricted to consciousness and defined perception as an organism responding to objects of the environment with regularities in behavior (Bartley, 1958). Moreover, McBurney and Collins noted that perceptual behavior was not a separate entity from cognate, emotional or other factors attributable to behavior.

Forgus and Malamed maintained that perception was the "process of information extraction (Forgus et. al. 1976, p. 12). Further, Hilgard viewed perception as a way of becoming aware of qualities, objects, and relations through the senses. Hilgard further suggested that sensory content was present in perceptions with prior experiences affecting how one perceived an organism (Edmonds, 1951, pp. 97–112).

Sherif (1954) stated that perception was influenced by psychological factors that were internal and external to individuals. Sherif further noted that "the totality of functionally related internal and external factors influenced perceptional structure" (Sherif, 1954, p. 18).

Farnsworth (1963) stated that cognitive and affective condition influenced an individual's perception. Farnsworth placed those conditions into five categories:

1. Sensitivity or effectiveness of an individual's organs;

2. Set prior experiences and the accompanying mental structure developed in each individual;

3. The ability to interpret new experiences by associating or relating them to past experiences;

4. The strength of the stimulus on the perceiver, and

5. The memory or ability to recall (Farnsworth, 1963, p. 18)

Perception and Selectivity

According to Howard Bartley, man is in the unique and peculiar position of having to "lift himself by his own bootstraps." Man needs to know about his environment and himself, but contrary to the logical necessity of the situation man confronts, man has no absolute starting point. That is, man possesses no absolute knowledge of his surroundings. However, man does possess his own sense organs, his own nervous system and his own effectors, the muscles. Yet these are the very mechanisms that man wants to test and understand. Thus, man can do no better than to use his faculties and abilities to experience and conceptualize and to make order out of his encounters (Bartley, 1980, p. 20).

Moreover, noted theorist Irvin Rock, distinguishes perception from other modes of cognition (such as imagination or dreaming or thought) in that perception is the mental representation of external objects and events that is based upon or perhaps in some way corresponds to the simulation reaching our sense organs (Rock, 1983, p. 28). So the term perception, then is the overall activity of the organism that immediately follows or accompanies energetic impingements upon the sense organs.

Furthermore, Rock, states that one can first separate theories of perception into two major categories depending upon whether specification of the relevant stimulus for every perception is deemed stimulus theory or the constructive theory in which the organism uses "internal processing" to transform the stimulus.

More specifically, stimulus theory states that for every distinct kind of perceptual property--of color, size, depth, movement, and the like--there is a unique stimulus reaching the sense organ. Rock states further that we may or may not know what that stimulus is, but if we do not, it is in principle discoverable. We may choose to call this correlation between stimulus and precept the explanation, or we may choose to further examine and ascertain the sensory processes that transduce the physical stimulus, encode it mentally and transmit it deeper into the brain (Rock, 1983, p. 28).

Conversely, the Gestalt Constructive Theory or spontaneous interaction theory states that the determinant of a perception is not the stimulus but spontaneous interaction between the representations of several stimuli or interaction between the stimulus and more central representations. That is, such interaction could only take place in a manner consistent with the known principles of neurophysiology. The essence of this theory is that more complex interactive events ensue following stimulation and can allow for known effects, such as those of context, constancy, contrast, perceptual changes without stimulus changes, illusions, and the like (Rock, 1983, p. 32).

The cognitive theory states that stimulus input is not so much transformed by spontaneous interaction as it is interpreted by higher cognitive agency outside the stimulus domain. In fact, the proximal state of affairs is available for such interpretation in a form not too different from its physical characteristics given in a retina image. Thus, the theory states that grouping is something imposed upon the unmodified proximal array by a cognitive agency, and enrichment results from the imposition of a description in the organized stimulus in terms of the properties of the known object (Rock, 1983, p. 40).

Of course, there are other current theories about perception, for example, selection, accentuation fixation, perceptual defense, perception, and subception. Perhaps the information processing, about perception analyzes the stages of processing that are assumed to occur from the moment of stimulation to the ultimate cognition, decision or action. As such, the approach seems to be theoretically neutral. However, depending upon the stage under analysis, one finds emphasis on aspects of each of the three theories. For example, one finds how the information about the proximal stimulus is explicated or extracted, how it remains available in that form, how this information may be transformed by processes, such as lateral inhibition, and how this in turn may be "recognized" or "interpreted" on the basis of rules devised from past experience.

Among the scholars cited, the conceptual framework of human values, attitudes, and perceptions were embedded in social, cultural, and political fabric of society. Thus, these cognitive and affective factors hinged on one's perceptual motors in one's view of other cultures. Thus the interaction of these variables played a key role in voters' perception of the 1990 U.S. Senate race between Harvey Gantt and Senator Jesse Helms.

Ball-Rokeach and DeFleur's Dependency Model Of Mass Communication Effects

Ball-Rokeach and DeFleur (1976) indicated that the structural conditions of a society were interwoven with mass media. In other words, Ball-Rokeach stated that mass media served as an "information system" that had a key role in maintenance, change, and conflict processes at the societal, group, and individual levels of social action.

Moreover, Ball-Rokeach and DeFleur's dependency model of mass communication effects noted that audience members of modern societies depended on the mass media for knowledge and orientation toward societal needs and governmental operations. The degree of dependency, however, corresponded to structural conditions within society--whether stable or unstable. The model also depicted the interrelation between three main variables: the societal system, the media system, and the audiences and specified certain effects, such as cognitive, affective, and behavior as a result of this inter-action. The cognitive effects dealt with the creation and resolution of ambiguity, attitude formation, agenda setting and expansion of people's system. The affective dealt with creating fear or anxiety and increasing or decreasing morale (alienation). Finally, the behav-ioral dealt with activation or de-activation, issue formation or issue resolution, reaching or providing strategies for action (e.g. political demonstration and causing altruistic behavior (e.g. donating money to charities). The authors noted that each component can change in ways which were relevant to the differential occurrence of effects.

For instance, the social system varied according to its degree of instability (developing countries). Hence, the social system's change or instability directly affected the survival of such a system in terms of attitudes, old values and re-asserted new ones--all of which stimulated information giving and receiving processes. For the audience, the relationships toward the social system varied. More specifically, some groups were to gain while others lost. A vivid example was the social elite group which had more control over the media, more access to them and also was less dependent on them. The social elite groups, then, had access to expert sources of information. On the other hand, the non-elites were heavily dependent on mass media or poorly informed personal sources. Finally, Ball-Rokeach and DeFleur (1976) indicated that the mass media varied in quantity, diversity, reliability and authority. The mass media in some societies provided more social or political information than in others.

A New Prospective:
Scholars and Philosophical Implications of Objectivity

The notion of objectivity in news coverage has been deeply rooted in Western thought and has been practiced in the Western journalism profession in the United States, going back to the Colonial era. In their early years, journalists believed that covering all views was evident of objectivity and unbiased coverage. Recently, scholars (Schadron, 1978) noted that achieving objectivity was virtually impossible because news stories were written from a reporter's perspective which added that personal element. Moreover, Schadron further purported that the mere selection process was subjective. Thus, the objectivity notion was replaced by notions of a reporter being fair, accurate and unbiased.

Hence, Hayakawa (1972), in stating that it was impossible for American journalists to attain complete impartiality, noted that by the mere process of selection and abstraction imposed on them by their own interests, background, and experience reflected news being slanted. Hayakawa further noted that objectivity was possible if journalists were aware of their biases and used this awareness to balance judgments, either favorable or unfavorable, in concert (Hayakawa 1972, pp. 42–45).

Moreover, the *Commission on Freedom of the Press* stated in 1947 that the press owed society truthful, intelligent, and comprehensive news. Gans (1979) further maintained that the goal of journalistic objectivity was to exclude preference statements about a nation or society in news reports (Siebert 1976, p 60; Gans 1979, p. 184).

In terms of philosophical approaches to objectivity, Merrill examined a realist's view and an idealist's view of objectivity. Merrill noted that the realist viewed objectivity as a relational concept between the event and the story. The realist was concerned with neutrality. On the contrary, the idealist viewed objectivity as a relational concept between the audience and the report. The idealist was concerned with perceptions in the minds of the subjects (Merrill, et al. 1983, p. 177).

McDonald (1971) noted that objectivity subsumed Mass Communication principles morally, artistically and intellectually. In other words, all journalists and their institutions that employed them were part of the process. Further, Gans (1978) noted that journalists debated the process of value exclusion and the process of exercising news judgments. Gans further stated that objectivity involved the journalist and news operation (McDonald 1971, p. 29; Gans 1979, p. 184).

Tuchman (1978) suggested that objectivity was a "strategic ritual" that journalists used to protect themselves from libelous court cases. Tuchman also believed that this "strategic ritual" was used offensively or defensively by reporters. In other words, this "strategic ritual" was manifested by the presentation of the inverted pyramid concept used amongst journalists.

Boyer stated, however, that despite the disagreement amongst some journalists, the majority of journalists supported "Objectivity" as a standard. In fact, Boyer examined fifty editors and found that their views swayed in terms of the practicality of objectivity; however, editors endorsed objectivity as a "standard" (Edmonds, 1951, pp. 220–222).

Merrill Stevenson and Green's Studies on Objectivity Concept

Based on Boyer's survey, editors endorsed objectivity as a standard. However, an early study conducted by Merrill examined *Time* coverage of presidents. Merrill's' content analysis found that *Time's* coverage of presidents Truman, Eisenhower, and Kennedy failed in terms of objectivity. In fact, Merrill's study stated that Time was subjective in its news coverage. Moreover, Merrill conducted a replication of this study ten years later and concluded the same results (Merrill 42:pp. 563–570).

In television, Williams stated that bias studies in news programs revealed unsound data. Williams examined four television studies in the 1970's and found scholars' inability to identify variables to determine the causation process.

Moreover, Stevenson and Greene in 1980 found new bias studies were inconsistent. The study indicated that the inconsistency was a direct result of researchers' inability to identify clear variables. Of equal importance, a study by Merron, et al. of former vice presidential candidate, Geraldine Ferraro, revealed no bias among the newspapers' coverage in Wisconsin.

Agenda-Setting Research: The Political Implications of News Coverage

The political implications of news coverage were evident in the mid-1800s. During this time that U.S. President Abraham Lincoln stated that public sentiment was everything and with public sentiment, nothing could fail. Further, President Lincoln stated that without public sentiment nothing could succeed. Lincoln's comments had deeper implications whereby the mass media played a key role (Rogers, et al. 1986, p. 555). However, political analyst Walter Lippmann in 1922 provided a conceptual framework of the agenda setting function, suggesting that the media were responsible for the "pictures in our heads."

Lang and Lang's study (1951) examined the MacArthur Day parade in which the television audience had a different impression than the spectators who attended the same event. Lang and Lang further stated that differences were accented by the medium's (television) technical limitations. Lang and Lang noted that television selected the interesting shots or salient events for its audience.

Boorstin's 1962 book, *The Image*, reinforced Lippmann's (1922) notion of agenda setting by the media. Boorstin illustrated his views about the media with a conversation between two mothers: "My, that's a beautiful baby you have there." The second mother responded, "Oh, that's nothing. You should see his photograph" (Boorstin 1962, p. 1).

However, Cohen (1963) further articulated the agenda setting concept. More importantly, Cohen's affirmation gave birth to the body of research that looked into the agenda-setting function of the press. Cohen stated "it [the press] was not successful much of the time in telling people what to think, but was stunningly successful in telling its readers what to think about" (Dominick et al. 1987, p. 385). In fact, Cohen's qualitative study contended that the press played a key role in the foreign policy process. Cohen referred to his process as "map making" in which it depicted a view of the world by virtue of news stories coverage. Cohen's study was based on interviews with current and former policy makers in the executive branch of the United States government (Cohen 1963, p. 13).

In 1966 Lang and Lang further assessed the media impact and stated that "the mass media forced attention to certain issues....They were constantly presenting objects, suggesting what individuals in the mass should think about, know about, have feelings about" (Dominick et al. 1987, p. 386).

Whiteside's investigation into the media, specifically television coverage of the 1968 Chicago Democratic Convention, gave a specific focus on television as a medium. Whiteside's examination revealed that television's selection of images within the environment determines the "reality" for its audience (Whiteside 1968-69, p. 33-54).

This cognitive world, or pseudo-environment images created by mass communicative beliefs about certain issues was illustrated when McCombs and Shaw conducted the first empirical test of agenda setting in 1972. The 1968 Chapel Hill election study focused on this cognitive world by scrutinizing the bits of selected information prioritized by each voter. Three dimensions of the cognitive worlds were studied:

> The amount of information gained from communication; the differentiation or degree of detail in that information; and the salience of information in terms of the cognitive images (McCombs et al 1969, p. 17). They found strong support for the agenda setting hypothesis. In fact, McComb's and Shaw's study revealed strong relationships between media agenda of important issues and voters'

judgement in relation to issues by mass communication and campaign topics.

Moreover, at the time McCombs and Shaw (1972) collected their data, mass communication research was changing from being a temporary pursuit of social psychologists (like Kurt Levin and Carl Hovland), political scientists (like Harold Lasswell), and sociologists (like Paul Lazarsfeld, to becoming a major concern for the new breed of Ph.D.'s who were emerging from schools of communication. Unlike the social scientists who were attracted to study communication, the new communication scholars had pre-doctoral experience in journalism or broadcasting, scientific training, statistical and quantitative research methods. Hence, the new breed had reason to believe that mass media effects were evidence based on their personal background, even though the scientific finding of the field's four founders indicated only minimal effects of the mass media (Rogers, et al. 1986). Hence McCombs' and Shaw's study inspired other researchers to use other empirical methods that would further explain the agenda-setting hypothesis during a political campaign or otherwise.

For example, Tipton et al. (1975) used a cross-lagged correlation to analyze a state-wide election in relation to the media impact on voters. Tipton's et al. cross-lagged study was a type of longitudinal study in which information was used from two difference variables and from the same sample at two different times. Moreover, Patterson and McClure (1976) examined the impact of television news and television commercials on agenda setting in 1972. Patterson and McClure concluded that television news had minimal impact on public awareness of issues; however, television advertising had a profound effect on the audience's awareness of candidates' positions on campaign issues (McComb and Shaw (1969), p. 17; Tipton, et al. (1975); Patterson and McClure, (1976).

At approximately the same time that McCombs and Shaw were developing their ideas of agenda setting, Cobb and Elder (1971 and

1972) were developing a new perspective in relation to the mass media. These authors took a myopic view in relation to media setting the agenda. In other words, Cobb and Elder examined "building," the process by which issues emerge as legitimate concerns of policy-makers. The emphasis here was on linkage and the interaction process of news making (Elder and Cobb, 1983).

Consonant with Elder's and Cobb's concept of the interactive process, Weaver and Elliott (empirical) studied the relationship of a news source, namely a municipal authority and a local paper. They concluded that the municipal authority was more than likely to set the agenda for the paper.

Megwa and Brenner analyzed the *Missouri House Journal*, the record of the 82nd General Assembly of the Missouri House of Representatives, and two newspapers that covered these political proceedings, the *St. Louis Post Dispatch*, and the *Columbus Daily Tribune*, for the year of 1983 and January through May 1987 for agenda items of importance.

In the study, Megwa and Brenner acknowledged that the mass media and government were two important and powerful institu-tions in society as producers of public knowledge and issues creators. From a source agenda setting perspective, Megwa and Brenner found that the Missouri state legislature did set the agenda for the media. Thus, Weaver's (1982) review of the media agenda-setting research in which he stated that "the press does not reflect reality, rather filters and shapes it" was apparent in this study. Moreover, Megwa's and Brenner's study thoroughly illustrated the conduit role by those two newspapers and raised new questions about objective reporting in regard to the traditional concepts. Did the media carry out the "movers' and shakers'" ideology (disregarding journalistic ethics)? What kinds of political pressures were given to these institutions (media)?

Perhaps, the Megwa's and Brenner's findings gave credence to a notable scholar, namely, Gandy (1982) who stated public issues and political decisions were not made based solely on knowledge and perception of issues but by other factors in which degrees of information were controlled. Gandy further posited that as a result of information controlled by powerful sources, a large part of society was not accounted for in terms of political participation.

Clearly, Megwa and Brenner and other scholars' studies offered new insights into the agenda setting and source setting concepts as well as probing the objectivity philosophy. Finally, Megwa's and Brenner's study revealed that the two newspapers played a role in dealing with the powerful institution (Missouri legislative body) and served as a conduit for the "political elite" (Megwa and Brenner, 1988).

Manheim's Agenda Dynamics Model

Manheim (1986) developed Agenda Dynamics, an integrative model that consisted of three distinct agendas. Those agendas were of the media, the public, and policymakers. Manheim further stated that each had its own characteristic internal dynamics, and each was connected to the other by information, behavioral, or institutional bridges.

For instance, the media agenda consisted of those issues, actors, events images and viewpoints that received time or space in newspapers or broadcast that were communicated to a given audience. The political content of the media agenda was determined through an interaction mechanism that consisted of journalistic norms and behaviors, organizational structures and constraints and communication between media representatives and potential newsmakers. Moreover, upon closer examination of the role of the media agenda in an integrated system of agenda dynamics, Manheim outlined three dimensions. The first is *Visibility*, in which any actor, event or object required a certain amount of prominence of coverage by the media. For instance, one dimension would be the president of the United States staging a press conference to convene with Americans. The second is *Audience Salience*, referred to as relevance of news content to audience needs, such as social stability and economic security. Manheim believed that the function of such content was to help members of the audience assimilate news. The third dimension is the media agenda, *Valence*, referred to as the sense of favor, neutrality, or to disfavor an audience viewed as a given object. Manheim believed that the portrayal of issues or actors influenced the public's perception, either negatively or positively.

In the case of the public agenda, Manheim outlined three dimensions that included *familiarity, personal salience*, and *favorability. Familiarity* referred to the degree of public awareness of or attention to a given topic. In other words, the audience's cognition played a role in discerning information. *Personal salience* referred to involvement, interest in or one's perceived relevance to a given topic. *Favorability*, on the other hand, represented the preference of an individual or a public in regard to an agenda item. Manheim stated, however, that the preference depended upon one's level of analysis (Manheim 1986).

In the case of the policy agenda, Manheim included the definition offered by Cobb et. al., who stated that policy agenda consisted of a "list of items which decision makers accepted for serious consideration." The authors outlined the ways in which issues moved on and off the policy agenda. First, they noted the likelihood that a governmental body's actions depended upon a given *actor* or *event*. Finally, the freedom of action referred to the responses or actions that were available to policymakers on a given question. Manheim believed that the positioning of issues on the media and public agendas was a component of an integrated system of agendas and agenda transfer (Cobb et al. 1976, p. 126; Manheim 1986, p. 507).

Source-Media Agenda-setting Model (Megwa and Brenner)

Megwa and Brenner developed "a paradigm of media agenda-setting" from a "source" perspective. In other words, Megwa and Brenner believed that the media acted as a conduit for powerful institutions in which those institutions set the media agenda. Thus, Megwa and Brenner used the "transactional model of communication" to examine the source-media interaction on the interpersonal and institutional levels. They believed that this method accounted for macro- as well as micro-dimensions of communication. Moreover, Megwa and Brenner believed that the source or initiator of communication in their "model" had a system of beliefs, and behavioral characteristics that he or she shared with the media. Hence, Megwa and Brenner's source-agenda setting model examined external forces that influenced the media such as press releases from large companies or agencies, press conferences and media events.

In the case of the media agenda, Megwa and Brenner stated three important stages that were used by constituencies: *Issue Creation* (Interest group), *Issue Expansion* (media), and *Issue Consumption.* Megwa and Brenner further posited that there were two distinct agendas. The Issue Creation stage had source and media; the Issue Expansion stage consisted of media, source and audience. Finally, the Issue Consumption consisted of audience, media, source, and policy (Megwa and Brenner, 1986). In the case of the source agenda, Megwa and Brenner believed that issues and topics (Information Subsidies) were used by the institutions or newsmakers to cajole the media in accepting their perspective as news. In other words, those institutions were in the "limelight" for that time again. Gandy (1982) viewed this process as information subsidies. Gandy further stated that by ("institutions") leading or controlling information those institutions had a profound influence on the receiver. Megwa and Brenner outlined three content dimensions: visibility, salience, and valence and three attributes or bridges: behavioral, information and

74

institutional in relation to the source agenda model (Gandy 1982, see Manheim 1986; Megwa and Brenner).

Agenda-setting Research: Future Directions and Implications

Iyengar and Kinder (1987) stated that agenda setting was an apt metaphor, but it was no theory. Rogers and Dearing (1986) reaffirmed this gloomy assessment at least in part, relative to agenda setting research studies. Roger and Dearing (1986) believed that agenda setting scholars devoted more time in conducting empirical investigations than theoretical developments. However, Rogers and Dearing (1986) acknowledged that the research activity moved toward improved measurement of media agendas, public agendas, and policy agendas; toward adequately processual aspects; and toward better statistical and analytical approaches for controlling "spurious relationships." Hence, Rogers and Dearing stated that agenda-setting research needed a thorough meta-research analysis more than another empirical study. Further, Rogers and Dearing proposed a three-by-three matrix that amended the "holes" in research on the media agenda, the public agenda, and the policy agenda. In fact, they cited nine possible relationships: the media's influence upon itself, the public, and policymakers; the public's influence upon itself, the media, and policymaker; and policymakers' and policymakers' and policymakers' influence upon themselves, the media, and the public. Moreover, they felt that a triangulation approach needed to be implemented for measuring public agendas (two or more different approaches) and cognitive processes. Finally, Rogers and Dearing proposed that future agenda-setting research dealing with "developing countries" and wider variability studies about agenda setting issues were of dire need (Rogers and Dearing 1986, p. 584).

Agenda Setting: Race, Southern Culture, and Race-Baiting Campaign Ads

The agenda setting philosophy states that the mass media provides the public with an array of political and social issues of public debate. The News media may give issues saliency; however, the media may not have direct influence on the public's cognitive and affective processes. In other words, the media makes the public think about issues of saliency in relation to their experiences (Salwen, et. al., 1997, p. 329).

McCombs (1992) notes that to view the agenda setting concept solely on a societal level is inappropriate, and he also asserts that researchers need to thoroughly examine the antecedents of issues of salience and that individuals' personal experiences are interwoven in their interest in societal problems.

Moreover, cultural research studies regarding race and Southern culture in the agenda-setting process indicate that the news production process reflects the dominant ideology, one which presents news events in a socially constructed perspective that appears to be rooted in what is "morally right or morally wrong". This hedgemonic process, however, is continuous among competitors of news producers for readers. Nevertheless, news is on the ideological apparatus and represents views of the ruling elite (Hall, 1977, 1982; Hartley, 1982; Gramsci, 1971, 1983; Hall, 1980; Althusser, 1971).

Of equal importance, critical research studies have found that the portrayal of African-Americans in the news in the United States is deeply interwoven in racial ideology. This social ideology is perpetuated by news coverage of issues and assumptions about African Americans: crime, poverty, and middle class success. These misrepresentations by news coverage underscore the notion that racial ideology is not interwoven in the elite's belief system (Hall, et.

al., 1978; Entman, 1990, 1992; Gray, 1989; Hartmann and Husband, 1974; Shah and Thorton, 1994; Van Dijk, 1991).

Montagu (1974) notes that racial ideology may be used synonymously with the term racism. Montagu asserts the term racism is interwoven in a system of beliefs which espoused certain connotations and understanding of race. More specifically, Montagu notes that the term racism as belief emphasizes that "natural or biological" races of mankind differ from one another mentally as well as physically. The traits of one's race, then, become essential elements in evoking one's superiority in term of one's biological differences based on pigmentation characteristics (Montagu, 1974, p. 14-18).

Brandt (1991) asserts that institutional racism has impacted social conditions more than bigotry or indifferences. Institutional racism empowers institutions to enforce prejudices. Van Dijk (1991) states that elite racism is mirrored by coverage of race because elites are owners and executives of news institutions which define the issues of saliency for races (Brandt, 1991; Van Dijk 1991; Williams, 1985).

Entman (1990-92) asserts that news representation of African Americans mirrored symbolic or modern racism to convey a negative sentiment among whites. He also notes that modern racism differed from traditional racism, which opponents had toward integration, equality, and accepted negative stereotypical images about African American intellectual aptitude. Schuman and Sears (1988) suggest that this symbolic racism and white social attitudes since 1942 had changed from overt to symbolic racism. In this conceptual framework, then, African Americans are viewed as violators of traditional American values, such as patriotism, individualism and self-reliance (Entman, 1990-92; Sears, 1988; McConahay, 1986; Schuman, et. al.,1985, p. 177; Myrdal, 1964, pp. 441-459).

McConahay (1982) notes that traditional or old fashioned racism is steeped in the United States until the era of Civil Rights in 1954. Within this time, traditional ideology is viewed as "the Southern defense ideology." Southern whites evoked a sense of pride of this benevolence toward Negro dependents but would resent vigorously their demanding this aid as a "right" (McConahay, 1982, p. 705; Myrdal, 1964, p. 441-459).

Meyers (1996) indicates that through racism or racial overtures, symbolic racism can be viewed as an institutional process as well as a human process within a historical or cultural context. Moreover, the news paradigm process shaped and mirrored the dominant paradigm of race. Hence, the issue of race and race relations then mirrored racial attitudes and stereotypes within the elite dominant paradigm of race (Meyers, 1996, p. 172; Hacker, 1992).

Jamieson (1992) notes that in the 1990 Senatorial race in North Carolina, Democrat Harvey Gantt appeared to be the front-runner during the final weeks. He further notes that Gantt's advisors thought that the issue of race and race-baiting ads did not exist. Voters and political pollsters indicate that Gantt's platform on education and environment was essential to most swing voters and supporters. However, Senator Helm's ads were visceral and provided an impetus for his supporters.

More specifically, Senator Helms' first "race priming ad" dealt with the issue of abortion. Senator Helms was against abortion and Gantt supports sex selection. Senator Helms' ad portrays Gantt as a prevaricator, liberal, stupid and the transformation of color video images to black and white, which created a darker pigmentation for viewers. A second ad portrays Gantt's African-American campaign manager denying charges by Senator Helms' campaigns ad maker with an "acoustically tinny" voice. Senator Helms' third ad deals with the integrity of Gantt. Helms' ad questions Gantt's using his mayoral influences and minority status to receive a free television license from the federal government. Helms' ad implies that Gantt sold his share to a white corporation to become a millionaire. The ad illustrates that Gantt's actions suggested selfishness and betrayal of the African-American community. The newspaper headlines, then, read "Gantt might make $3 million by selling TV Station" (emphasis added) (Jamieson, 1992, p. 97).

Jamieson notes that the final ad had a major impact on swing voters. Helms' ad makers displayed plaid-shirted arms and white hands being rejected for a job. The announcer emphasizes that "you needed that job and you were the best qualified. But they had to give it to a minority because of racial quota. Is that really fair? Harvey Gantt says it is. Gantt supports Ted Kennedy's racial quota law that makes the color of your skin more important than your qualifications. Cast your vote on this issue next Tuesday. For racial quotas: Harvey Gantt; Against racial quotas: Jesse Helms" (Jamieson, 1992, p. 97).

The issue of race and race-baiting campaigns, traditional racism, and modern racism symbolized coded language used during Democratic Harvey Gantt and Republican incumbent Jesse Helms' campaigns.

Senator Helms won with 52.5 percent of the vote. Jamieson noted that the state of North Carolina listed 2,677,162 North Carolinians as "white" and 635,045 as "African-American." Gantt, who needed 42 percent of the white votes, received 38 percent or 981,573 votes (Jamieson, 1992, p. 94).

An examination of newspaper coverage, *News and Observer* and the *Charlotte Observer* coverage of Harvey Gantt and Senator Jesse Helms, should bring forth new insights into political campaigns.

Hypotheses

> Hypothesis 1: Harvey Gantt received less favorable coverage than Senator Jesse Helms based on race.

Hypothesis 2: Harvey Gantt received less favorable newspaper coverage than Senator Jesse Helms on the agenda of substantive attributes of candidates (e.g. personality, their stand on social and political issues).

Hypothesis 3: Harvey Gantt received less favorable newspaper coverage than Senator Jesse Helms on the agenda of affective attributes of candidates (e.g. courage, natural intelligence, honesty).

	Race N&O	Total		Charlotte	Total
Gantt			**Gantt**		
July	12%	0.12	July	9%	0.09
Aug	20%	0.2	Aug	13%	0.13
Sept	24%	0.32	Sept	22%	0.22
Oct	36%	0.36	Oct	38%	0.38
Nov	8%	0.08	Nov	18%	0.18
July	7%	0.07			
Aug	12%	0.12			
Sept	27%	0.19			
Oct	39%	0.39			
Nov	15%	0.15			
Helms			**Helms**		
July	20%	0.2	July	7%	0.07
Aug	20%	0.2	Aug	12%	0.12
Sept	0%	0.4	Sept	27%	0.19
Oct	20%	0.2	Oct	39%	0.39
Nov	40%	0.4	Nov	15%	0.15
July	9%	0.09			
Aug	13%	0.13			
Sept	22%	0.22			
Oct	38%	0.38			
Nov	18%	0.18			

Hypothesis 2 (Gantt)

		Hypothesis 2 (Gantt)	
Liberal	33.30%	Liberal	46.90%
Tax Income	14.60%	Tax Income	29.60%
Proposal Program	29.20%	Proposal Program	42%
Oppose Death Penalty	14.60%	Oppose Death Penalty	11.10%
Education	43.80%	Education	59.30%
Pro Art	6.30%	Pro Art	13%
Health Care	29.20%	Health Care	44.40%
Pro Environment	31.30%	Pro Environment	49.40%

Hypothesis 2 (Helms)

		Hypothesis 2 (Helms)	
Against Education	27.10%	Against Education	28.40%
Against Health	12.50%	Against Health	27.20%
Conservative	20.80%	Conservative	30.90%
No Tax Increase	12.50%	No Tax Increase	25.90%
Against Social Programs	27.10%	Against Social Programs	43.20%
Support Death Penalty	16.70%	Support Death Penalty	7.40%
Against Art	14.60%	Against Art	21%
Against Environment	25%	Against Environment	30.90%

Hypothesis 3 (Gantt)

		Hypothesis 3 (Gantt)	
Patriotic	2%	Patriotic	7%
Trustworthy	6%	Trustworthy	7%
N.C. Values	16.60%	N.C. Values	7%
Dishonest	19%	Dishonest	22%

Hypothesis 3 (Helms)

		Hypothesis 3 (Helms)	
Patriotic	6%	Patriotic	17%
Trustworthy	6%	Trustworthy	15%
N.C. Value	19%	N.C. Value	15%
Dishonest	23%	Dishonest	27%

Hypothesis 4 (Gantt)

Inexperienced Campaign Manager	14.60%
Instate Campaign Finance	19%
Out-of-State Campaign	35%
Campaign Spending	17%
No Political Connectedness	8%
Less Powerful	19%

Hypothesis 4 (Helms)

Experienced Campaign Manager	10%
Instate Campaign Finance	15%
Out-of-State Campaign Finance	19%
More Campaign Spending	8%
Political Connetedness	31%
Powerful/Incumbent	2%

Hypothesis 4 (Gantt)

Inexperienced Campaign Manager	27%
Instate Campaign Finance	36%
Out-of-State Campaign	33%
Campaign Spending	20%
No Political Connectedness	19%
Less Powerful	0%

Hypothesis 4 (Helms)

Experienced Campaign Manager	30%
Instate Campaign Finance	31%
Out-of-State Campaign Finance	20%
More Campaign Spending	26%
Political Connetedness	31%
Powerful/Incumbent	28%

Chapter Four

Content Analysis: A Research Methodology

Content analysis in communication research can bring high reliable results if content analysis techniques are used objectively, systematically, quantitatively in analyzing manifest content (Stempel, 1981: 119-120). Communication scholars consider content analysis as one of the most important methodological tools used in conducting communication research. Various definitions of content analysis abound among scholars. For instance, Walizer and Wienir (1978) have defined content analysis as any systematic procedure which examines recorded information. Krippendorf (1980) maintains that content analysis is a research methodology for making replicating studies and drawing valid inferences from data to their context. Kerlinger (1980) defines content analysis as a method of studying and analyzing communication data systematically, objectively, and quantitatively in measuring variables.

Kerlinger further notes that "systematical" means that the content is to be analyzed according to consistent rules. That is, the sample selection must be properly administered, and each variable must have an equal chance to be selected for analysis. Moreover, Kerlinger notes that the evaluation process must be systematic and that the coding process must have uniformity. The term "objective", notes Kerlinger, is that the personal, idiosyncratic biases of the principal investigator are included in the analysis. Thus, if the study is replicated by another researcher, the same results should occur. Hence, the operational definitions and rules for classifying variables must be lucid and comprehensive for other researchers replicating that study. Finally, Kerlinger (1980) notes that "quantitative" means providing measurable information to principal researchers with precision. Quantification then, allows researchers to analyze results and report them with a greater certainty. Of equal importance, quantification provides researchers with statistical methods to aid them in interpreting analysis (Dominick and Wimmer, 1987, p. 166).

Berelson (1952) provided a classic definition of content analysis methodology. He indicated that the key to understanding content analysis and implementing it lies in fully understanding the meaning of objective, systematic, quantitative, and manifest content. According to Berelson, content analyses can be viewed as follows:

> *Objective...* means the opposite of subjective or impressionistic. Objectivity is achieved in a content analysis study by defining the categories for replication purposes. If content were subjective instead of objective, each researcher would have his own content analysis. Thus, objective means that the results depend upon the procedure and not the analyst.
>
> *Systematic...* means that a set of procedures is applied in the same way to all the content being analyzed. Second, it means that categories are set up so that relevant content

is analyzed. Finally, it means that analyses are designed to secure data relevant to a research question or hypothesis.

Quantitative... means recording the numerical values or the frequencies with which the various defined types of content occur.

Manifest Content... means the apparent content, which means that content must be coded as it appears rather than as the content analyst feels it is intended.

Additionally, Stempel specified four methodological problems that a researcher must confront in undertaking a content analysis study: Selection of the unit of analysis, category construction, sampling of content, and reliability of coding (Stempel, 1981).

The Implementation of Content Analysis Methodologies

In the early 1940's, political analyst Lasswell and cohorts formulated procedures in evaluating political coverage of newspapers. Lasswell (1942) noted, however, that there was not an absolute tool which would provide lucid answers on every political communication study of the press. Hence, Lasswell, et. al. (1942) proposed the following procedures in analyzing political newspaper content:

1. Select the symbol list

2. Define the list

3. Select the unit and construct categories for analysis

4. Train coders for data reliability

5. Analyze data and draw conclusions

Sampling

Krippendorf (1980) noted that communication has always imbued the lives of human beings. However, the new inventions within the print, broadcast as well as electronic computer communication added new dimensions in the availability of symbolic material. Krippendorf further stated that these instructions produced a large volume of information in which a content analyst must employ a tool to manage such a size.

In other words, the content analyst must select sampling procedures to reduce large volumes of potential data to a manageable size. Thus, sampling processes emanated from a sampling plan which entailed specifics as to the way the study would be implemented. Of equal importance, the sampling plan assured no biases and equal representative of the population to be sampled. The content analyst was responsible for the sample plan results (Krippendorf, 1980, p. 66).

Moreover, Krippendorf noted different types of sampling schemes for a content analyst to utilize in examining political newspaper content, for instance, random sampling, stratified samplings, systematic sampling, cluster sampling, varying probability sampling, and multistage sampling. Krippendorf noted that random sampling may not always be applicable (Krippendorf, 1980, p. 66).

Categorizing

The Categorization Process

Dominick and Wimmer (1987) noted that the categorization process was virtually important in the implementation of a content analysis study. They further implied that the composition of this

86

system varied with the research topic under evaluation (Dominick and Wimmer, 1987, p. 176-77).

However, Dominick and Wimmer (1987) posited that all category systems must be mutually exclusive, exhaustive, and reliable. Clearly, then, Dominick and Wimmer stated that any category system was mutually exclusive if the variable can be placed in one category only. Hence, if variables were not explicit and overlapped into other categories, then those questionable categories must be revised by the content analyst.

In addition to categories or partitions being exclusive, Dominick and Wimmer (1987) stated that the inclusion of exhaustivity within a content analysis study was of utmost importance. In other words, explicit categories as a whole were accountable for every unit of analysis within a content analysis study (Dominick and Wimmer, 1987, p. 177).

Krippendorf (1980) coined the term "exhaustivity" in categories with data languages and further acknowledged that "exhaustive" referred to the data language representative of unit analysis; hence, the data language being mutually exclusive was its ability to make lucid distinctions of variables under examination. Additionally, categories and measurements of connectedness with the real phenomena yielded scientific data and analytical "success" (Krippendorf, 1980, p. 85).

Moreover, Kerlinger (1986) outlined five vital rules for the categorization process:

1. Categories must be set up according to the research problem and purpose.

2. Categories must be exhaustive.

3. Categories must be mutually exclusive and independent.

4. Each category (variable) must be derived from one classification principle.

5. Any categorization must be on one accord (Kerlinger, 1986, p. 127).

Coding Process

Dominick and Wimmer (1987) noted that a unit of analysis placed into a content category was coding. A more scientific definition of coding was illustrated by Holsti (1969), who stated that coding was a process which placed systematically analyzed raw data into units for precision of content characteristics. Holsti further revealed that coding rules were connected to data and hypotheses and served as a vital part for the content analyst's design. Thus, according to Holsti, the content analyst must clearly define the research problem in terms of categories. Moreover, the content analyst must specify the unit of content to be categorized and implement a system approach for the enumeration process (Dominick and Wimmer, 1987; Holsti, 1969).

In addition, Geller, Kaplan and Lasswell (1942) outlined four methods for codifying newspaper content. Those methodologies were as follows:

	Specified	
Method	Recording Unit	Content
1	symbol	Sentence
2	paragraph	paragraph
3	3 sentences	3 sentences
4	Article	Article

Krippendorf emphasized the importance of codifying data in the following excerpt:

Recording was one of the basic methodological problems in the social sciences and humanities. The preparation, accepted in the natural sciences, that reality was not accessible as such, except through the medium of a meaning instrument, applied here as well. One cannot analyze what was not suitably recorded, and one cannot expect that source material came cast in the formal terms of a data language. Recording was required whenever the phenomena of interest were either unstructured relative to the methods that were available or symbolic in the sense that they carry information about phenomena outside physical manifestations (Krippendorf, 1980, p. 71).

Of equal importance, Dominick, et. al. (1987) noted that experienced coders were vital in any content analysis process. Thus, coders were to be properly trained; however, they were not attuned to the content analyst's operational definition and category schemes. Moreover, the content analyst provision for such a training process for coders provided intercoder reliability which represented lucid and realistic data for reliability purposes (Dominick and Wimmer, 1987, p. 179).

Reliability and Validity

Dominick and Wimmer (1987) noted that the notion of reliability was of utmost importance in the implementation of a content analysis study. They further noted that if content analysis were to be considered objective, then its measures and procedurals must be reliable. Hence, they acknowledged that the term reliability was achieved through the repetition of the same materials which yield consistency in conclusion or results. Dominick et. al. proposed three steps in which reliability can be achieved. They stated that the content analyst defined category boundaries:

1) define category boundaries with maximum detail

2) train coders

3) conduct a pilot study

Holsti (1969) believed that agreement reliability amongst the content analyst and coders provide reliability. Contrarily, category reliability meant that lucid categories must be present if coders are to be on one accord in classifying items in appropriate categories with consistency. Krippendorf (1980) emphasized that the utilization of a reliable procedure must yield the same results from a particular set of phenomena. Krippendorf further noted three types of reliability:

1) Stability was the degree to which a process was invariant.

2) Reproductivity was the degree to which a process can be recreated under varying circumstances, at different locations, using different coders.

3) Accuracy was the degree to which a process functionally conforms to a known standard or yields what it was designed to yield (Krippendorf, 1980, p. 131).

On the contrary, validity was referred to the degrees to which an instrument measured what it was designed to measure. Moreover, "validity" then, epitomized a certain quality of research results which one can accept as "indisputable facts". In other words, the term "indisputable facts" was closely associated with "empirical truth," "predictive accuracy", and consistency with "established knowledge". Kerlinger (1986) cited varied types of validation processes:

1) Content validity was the representativeness or sampling adequacy of the content - the substance, the matter, the topic - of a meaning instrument.

2) Criterion - related validity and validation was a process in which tests or scale scores comparison with one or more external variables, or criteria, known or believed to measure the attribute under study.

3) Construct validity and construct validation were used to connect psychometric notions and practices to theoretical notions. Thus, construct validity was different from other

types of validity, because it was interwoven with theory, theory constructs and scientific empirical inquiry in testing of hypothesized relations. Thus, construct validity was scientifically important in modern measurement theory and practice (Kerlinger, (1986, p. 417-21).

The Importance of Computer Utilization in Content Analysis

Fred Kerlinger noted that computer utilization in content analysis had a profound effect on the way content analysts processed their data. Other scholars stated that many social scientists were lucid toward utilization of the content analysis methodology because computers made it easier for coding as well as data tabulations of large amounts of information. In fact, Budd, et. al (1967) noted that three categories exist in using computers in a content analysis study: (1) The reduction of statistical data, (2) Hypothesis and relationship differentiations, (3) Hypothesis testability (Budd, et. al, 1967, pp. 92-95).

Another computer approach used was the general inquiry which analyzed statistical analysis of verbal content. Stone described this approach thusly.

> ...a set of computer programs to identify systematically, within text, instances of words and phrases that belong to categories specified by the investigator, (b) occurrences and specified co-occurrences of categories, (c) provide a print and graph tabulations, (d) provide statistical test analysis, (e) arrange and re-arrange sentence structure according to category specification. In 1964, Holsti utilized this approach in examining political content (Holsti, 1964, pp. 382-88).

Moreover, Marquerite Fischer (1966) emphasized the key word in context approach. Fischer noted that this approach analyzed words instead of concepts. In other words, a content analyst extracted words from the title (slug) abstract or tests and indexed those words accordingly. For instance, Danielson and Jackson were instrumental in the further development of KWIC system. In 1963, Danielson and Jackson produced a computer system that scanned verbal content and listed twenty "key concepts" and provided a printout of 119 additional computer words. Hence, the Associated Press developed a mechanism involving the interaction of the computer with punch tape from the Associate Press teletypesetter. Consonant with the Associated Press, Wilhoit and Sherrill used computer analysis for their content analysis on U.S. senator's visibility on wire copy. Wilhoit and Sherrill were concerned with the computer recognizing 100 words (senators). Additionally, Holsti developed a system for using the computer with Osgood's "evaluative assertion analysis". Holsti was successful in the enumeration process and the numerical value category of each "evaluative adjective" (Wilhoit and Sherrill, 1968, p. 42-48; Holsti, 1969).

Finally, the success of a computer content analysis process was underpinned in the content analyst's ability to deal with data and objectives of the study in a consistent way but not with total rigidity. In other words, the content analyst's data analysis process usually needed adjustments. It was virtually impossible for any content analyst to perceive every problem (Stempel, et. al, 1981, p. 131).

Conclusion

The media, to some degree, influences our perception and increases our knowledge of salient political issues. The media's role then is the creation, perpetuation and the transmission of values and images which directly or indirectly affect our attitudinal predisposition in a technological complex and historic racially stratified society.

Previous research has shown public awareness of media power and information control to expand the creation of political agendas and perpetuate values and beliefs of a dominant society. Thus, the dearth of literature on African American politicians and a systematic structural imbalance in the media hinders African Americans from effectively utilizing the media to engender their issues of saliency.

More specifically, the history of African American coverage by mainstream media depicted the cultural aspects and the race in a negative perspective. This negative imagery of African Americans, in general, and African American politicians, in particular, has permeated the social and political fabric of society.

In the wake of the decline of race dialogue and political race stratagem, the political climate and media race baiting campaigns have affected the electability and legitimacy of African American politicians.

Journalists in consonant with media owners then have shaped the image of political candidates and affected their behavior through their probing queries for voters. The portrayal of a candidate's legitimacy affects a candidate's media accessibility and financial resources for campaign stability. The examination of such a powerful North Carolina political figure as Senator Jesse Helms played a key role in whether candidate Harvey Gantt received favorable coverage in a Democratic liberal media.

To examine the role of newspaper coverage, the *Raleigh News and Observer*, located in Raleigh, North Carolina (the state capital), and the *Charlotte Observer*, located in Charlotte, North Carolina (the largest city in North Carolina) were analyzed for content through the May and November 1990 Senatorial race.

Three hypotheses were developed out of three research questions. Each of these hypotheses will be examined.

> Hypothesis 1: Harvey Gantt received less favorable
> coverage than Senator Jesse Helms based
> on race. This hypothesis was supported

93

by data analysis in Chapter 5. The issue of race has transcended political candidates in the American Diaspora for centuries, particularly, in the South. The Senatorial race between Harvey Gantt and Jesse Helms substantiated a tradition embedded in North Carolina racial politics. The issue of race was a factor, however, the coverage of news articles of Senator Helms with strong roots and small town traditions in the state of North Carolina and his rise to a powerful senator was even more of a factor. Gantt was portrayed as a historic figure, but he had no roots in growing up in the state of North Carolina. Specifically, the percentage of references to race in articles relating to the contest between Harvey Gantt and Senator Jesse Helms was analyzed in *The News and Observer*. In the month of November the percentage of articles mentioning race was most relevant. Senator Jesse Helms' coverage of stories in *The News and Observer* was July 20%, August 20%, September 0%, October 20%, and November 40%; Harvey Gantt's was July 12%, August 20%, September 24%, October 36% and November 8%. This hypothesis was supported by the data analysis in Chapter 5.

Hypothesis 2: Gantt received less favorable newspaper coverage than Senator Helms on the agenda of substantive attributes of candidates (e.g. personality, their stand on social and political issues). Gantt received less favorable coverage than Senator Helms on substantive attributes. Furthermore, Gantt was continuously labeled as a liberal with liberal values and data indicated 33% (*News & Observer*) and 47% (*Charlotte Observer*). Contrarily Helms was labeled as a conservative and received 20% of the news coverage by the *News and Observer* and 31% by the *Charlotte Observer* (see Chart 2.0)

Hypothesis 3: Harvey Gantt received less favorable newspaper coverage than Senator Jesse Helms on the agenda of affective attributes of candidates (e.g. courage, natural intelligence, honesty). Gantt received less favorable coverage on affective issues than Senator Helms. Gantt received an affective attributer such as patriotic (2%), North Carolina values (17%), compared to Senator Helm's patriotic attributes (6%), and North Carolina values (19%) in the News and Observer. *The Charlotte Observer's* coverage of Harvey Gantt shows affective attributes such as patriotic values (7%), and North Carolina values (7%) in comparison to Senator Helms' patriotic values (17%) and North Carolina values (15%) (See chart 3.0).

In summary, racial political appeal campaigning and substantive issues were supported. The role of the media in setting the agenda and providing the public with an array of political and racial issues for public debate during the political campaign is indicative to its influence on society. More specifically, the media's role in the Harvey Gantt and Senator Jesse Helms' campaign in 1990 did reflect variations from previous studies of the media and the issue of race. However, this study elaborated on Southern cultures which symbolize racial tone and institutional racism to some degree which contributed to voter participation. In fact, cultural studies regarding the issue of race relative to the agenda-setting process indicates the media news coverage reflected the dominant ideology. Thus, the importance then of this study notes that studies relative to African American politicians, in particular, were misrepresented with negative images.

Future research may examine the dynamics of news media, owners' attitudes and journalists' in-depth coverage of the candidates' discussion on issues. For instance, researchers in mass media should examine journalists' edited versions of news stories by candidates during issues campaign forums.

Hypothesis 2

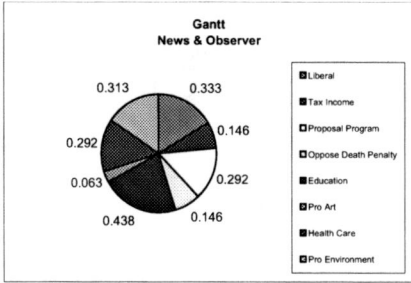

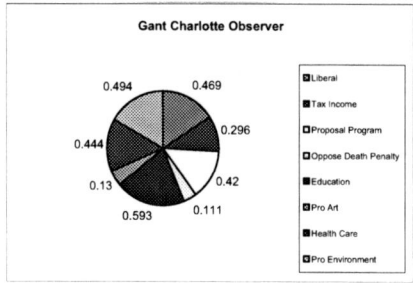

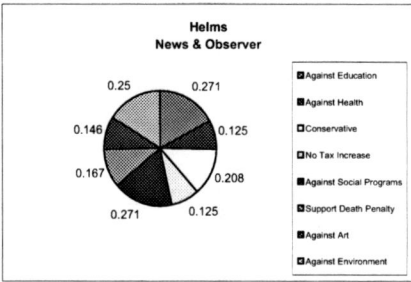

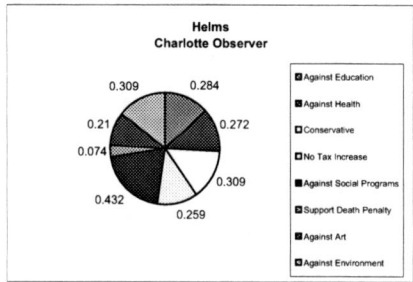

Hypothesis 3

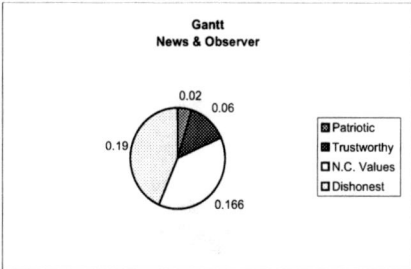

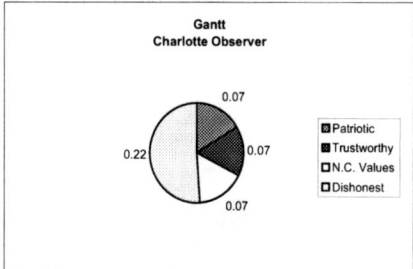

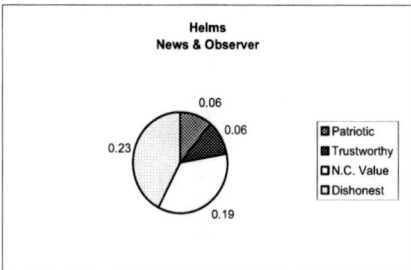

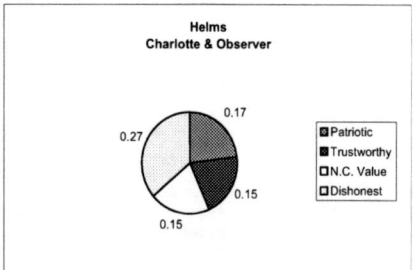

Exhibit Chart

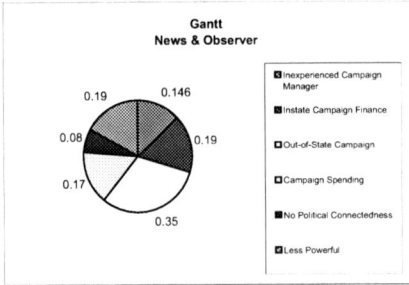

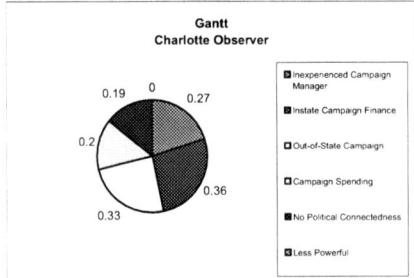

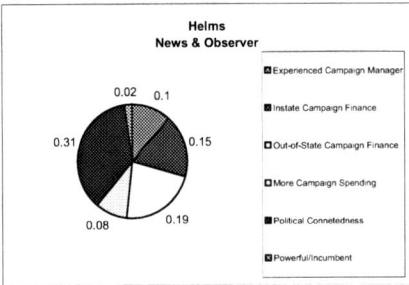

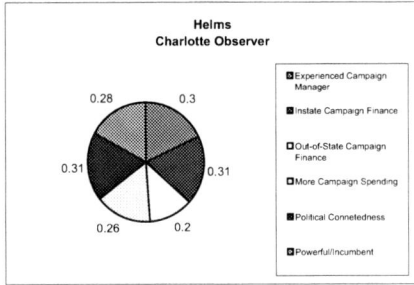

Hypothesis 1

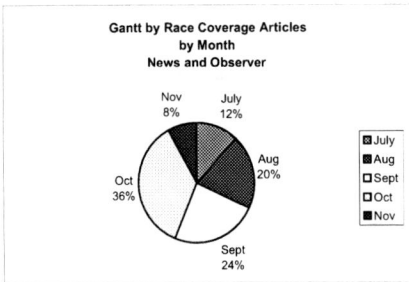

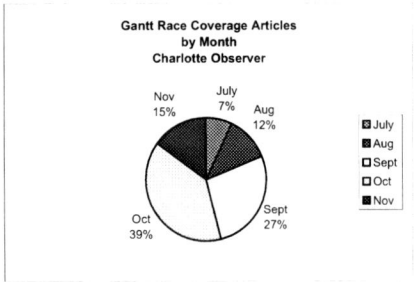

Chapter Five

Recommendations

It is vitally important for the leaders of the Democratic Party to champion its platform and support its nominee, irrespective of gender or race. The Democratic Party preamble notes the importance of fairness, diversity, inclusiveness and compassion. However, the senatorial race between Democratic nominee Harvey Gantt and incumbent Senator Jesse Helms revealed that Democrats' loyalty did not prevail. In fact, Democrats did not vote a straight ticket, and some cast their votes for the Republican incumbent Senator Jesse Helms. The issue of race preferences must be eradicated and party loyalty must become *deeds* not *words* in the case of electing democratic nominees to office, whether they are African Americans or of other origins.

Of equal importance, campaign resources for candidates, particularly African-American candidates must be accessible and all party supporters must play a key role in securing funds. That is, poor campaign resources make it virtually impossible to place issues of saliency in the media.

Moreover, the media-oriented process toward race legitimacy of a candidate must be examined. Of equal importance, the issue of race-baiting campaign ads must be discussed within the Democratic Party and the Republican Party platform leaders.

The issue of race-baiting campaigns throughout history has alarmed the citizenry of our great state and nation for too long. The divisiveness of racial ads from a societal perspective must be dealt with, especially the use of stereotypes and gory myths for the expediency of one's political party. Americans, old and young, in particular, have been often bombarded with images, lies, myths, beliefs which have affected their cognitive and affective behavior regarding certain cultures. However, if the American political system is to move toward a more effective system, race-baiting campaigns must be eliminated from the political campaign process.

Finally, the era of Reconstruction depicted the race issue as an important part of the American psyche. The 21st century, however, must be an era ushering in a new democratic platform for each party. A new heritage must be etched in the American psyche beyond that of political campaigns of the past. In the 21st century the coverage of candidates and the concerns of journalism must make the journalist's objectivity concept a reality. Thus, the cornerstones of an effective campaign must be issues oriented to ameliorate societal problems, not race-baiting which has only deepened racial stereotypes.

About the Author

Tony L. Powell, CEO/President of Powell Communications Enterprises, graduated with honors from Shaw University, earned his Master of Education degree from Virginia State University and has completed the coursework and dissertation for the Ph.D. at Howard University.

With a diverse background in communications, he has served as professor, executive producer, media specialist, as well as university spokesperson and public relations counsel at four University of North Carolina-system universities and other institutions of higher learning in other states.

As a man concerned with challenges facing today's youth, he has worked with programs, such as TRIO, to provide teaching, mentoring, and life skills development for students. In recognition of his service in the media and within the community, Powell has received an Outstanding Award for Educative/Sports Video Productions and Certificate of Recognition for the Jefferson Award from WTVD News Channel 11 ABC. In 1980 he received the Order of the

Long Leaf Pine Award from the North Carolina Governor's Office. He has been recipient of a Howard University Graduate Fellowship and a Faculty Summer Grant from the National Endowment for the Humanities at Georgetown University. In 2005 Powell was honored with the Shaw University Distinguished Alumnus Award.

Tony Powell continues his involvement with the media through his communications enterprise and expresses his commitment to serve his community in a variety of ways.

Bibliography

Ahearn, L. (1990, Oct. 21). Senate race: Two very public men fight for starbilling: Gantt long has been at ease as a symbol of change. *Greensboro News and Record.*

Albritton, R.B. & Manheim, J.B. (1985). Public relations efforts for the third world: Images in the News. *Journal of Communication* (winter), pp. 43-59.

Allport, F. (1955). *Theories of Perception and the Concept of Structure.* New York: John Wiley and Sons.

Allport, G.W. (1961). *Pattern and Growth in Personality.* New York: Holt, Rinehart, and Winston.

Althusser, L. (1971). Ideology and ideological state apparatuses. In *Lenin and Philosophy and Other Essays.* (pp. 127-186). New York: Monthly Review Press.

Babington, C. (1990, Nov. 7) Helms fans are exultant: GOP chief calls win a major breakthrough. *The News and Observer,* p.15A.

Babington, C. (1990, Oct. 31) Helms' values stem from small-town life. *The News and Observer.*

Ball-Rokeach, S. & DeFleur, M.L. (1976). A dependency model of mass media effects. *Communication Research, 3,* 3-21.

Barber, J.T. & Gandy, O.H. Jr. (1990). "Press Portrayal of African American and White United States Representatives." *The Howard Journal of Communications,* Vol. 2, No. 2, p. 213.

Barker, L. & McCorry, J. Jr. (1976). *Black Americans and the Political System.* Cambridge, MA: Winthrop Publishers.

Bartley, H. S. (1958). *Principles of Perception.* New York: Harper and Brothers.

Bartley, H. S. (1980). *Introduction to Perception.* New York: Harper Row.

Bass, J. & DeVries, W. (1977). *The Transformation of Southern Politics, Social Change and Political Consequence since 1945.* Basic Books.

Becker, L.E. (1982). Citizen assessment of issue importance: A reflection of an agenda-setting research. In D.C. Whitney E. Wartella and S. Windahl (eds.), *Mass Communication Review Yearbook,* Vol. 2, pp. 521-36.

Bell, L.S. (1973). *The role and performance of black and metro newspapers in relation to political campaigns in selected, racially mixed congressional elections:* 1960-1970. Unpublished doctoral dissertation, Northwestern University, Evanston.

Bennett, L. W. (1988). *The Politics of Illusion,* 2nd ed., New York: Longman.

Bennett, L., Jr. (1985). *Before the Mayflower: A History of Black America.* New York: Penguin.

Bennett, L., Jr. (1975). *The Shaping of Black Americans.* Chicago, IL: Johnson Publishing Company.

Berelson, B. (1952). *Content analysis in communication research.* New York: Free Press.

Bernstein, B. (1981). *Class, codes, and control.* London and Boston: Routledge and Kegan Paul.

Bittner, T.R. (1985). *Broadcasting and telecommunication.* Englewood Cliffs, NJ: Prentice Hall.

Black Democratic Registration Higher. *Associated Press.* (1990 Oct. 20) In *The Charlotte Observer.*

Black, E. & Black, M. (1987). *Politics and society in the south.* Cambridge, MA: Harvard University Press.

Black elected officials: a national roster. (1989). Joint Center for Political Studies, 18 ed. Washington, DC.

Boorstin, D. (1962). *The image,* New York: Athenaeum.

Boyer, J. H. How Editors View Objectivity. *Journalism Quarterly.* 58:24-28.

Brandt, J. (1991). *Dismantling racism: the continuing challenge to white America.* Minneapolis, MN: Augsburg Fortress.

Brisbane, R H. (1970). *The black vanguard: origins of the Negro social revolution 1900-1960.* Valley Forge:PA: Judson Press.

Broh, C.A. (1987). *A Horse of a Different Color: Television's Treatment of Jesse Jackson's Presidential Campaign.* Joint Center for Political Studies. Washington, D.C.

Bryant, J. & Zillmann, D. (1986). *Perspectives on Media Effects.* Hillsdale, NJ: Lawrence Erlbaum Associates.

Budd, R., Thorp, R.K., & Donohew, L. (1967). *Content analysis of communications.* MacMillan Company.

Carterette, E.C., et al. (1978). *Handbook of perception.* New York: Academic Press.

Caws, P. (1967). *Science and the theory of value.* New York: Random House.

Chaffe, S.H. (1987). *Assumptions and issues in communication science.* In Berger and S. Chaffe (ed.), *Handbook of Communication Science.*

Chaffe, S. (1975). *Political communication: issues and strategies for research.* California: Sage Publication.

Chaudhary, A.T. (1980). Press portrayal of black officials. *Journalism Quarterly*, 57:636-641.

Christensen, R. (1990, Nov. 7) Gantt's edge in urban areas not enough. *The News and Observer*, p. IA.

Christensen, R (1990, Oct. 31) Gantt, Helms keep attacks at a boil: Senator assails civil rights bills. *The News and Observer.*

C1endinen, D. (1988). *The prevailing south: life and politics in a changing culture.* Atlanta: Longstreet Press.

Cobb, R.W. & Elder, C.E. (1972). *Participation in American Politics: The dynamics of agenda-building.* Boston: Allyn and Bacon.

Colburn, D.R. & Lander, J.L. (1995). *The African American heritage of Florida.* Gainesville, FL: University Press of Florida.

Conrad, E. *The invention of the Negro.* (1969). New York: Paul S. Eriksson.

Conyers, J. E. & Wallace, W.L. (1976). *Black elected officials.* New York: Russell Sage.

Danielson, W., & Jackson, H.L. Magnetic tape context scanner program. A program note (No 98) for the Computation Center, University of North Carolina, Chapel Hill, NC: Computation Center, 1963.

Dates, J.L. & Gandy, O. (1985). How ideological constraints affect coverage of the Jesse Jackson campaign. *Journalism Quarterly*, 62:595-600.

Democratic Handbook, 1898. (1898) Raleigh, NC: Edwards and Broughton.

Dlahrendorf, R. (1959). *Class and class conflict in industrial society.* Palo Alto, CA: Stanford Press.

Dodd, S. (1950). *How to measure values.* University of Washington Research Study 18:166-168.

Dominick, J.E. & Wimmer, R.D. (1987). *Mass media research.* Belmont, CA: Wadsworth Publishing Company.

Drescher, J. (1990, Oct. 27) Donations to Gantt increase: Helms still alludes in fund raising. *The Charlotte Observer.*

Drescher, J. (1990, Oct. 27) Senate foes share business background: Leaders divided over who'd be better. *The Charlotte Observer.*

Drescher, J. & Wrinn, J. (1990, Oct. 27) Get votes out, Helms urges; the other side is going to. *The Charlotte Observer* .

Duncan, R. (1994). *Entrepreneur for equality: Governor Rufus Bullock, Commerce, and Race in Post-Civil War Georgia.* Athens and London: The University of Georgia Press.

Dymally, M. (1971). *Black politician: his struggle for power.* Belmont, CA: Wadsworth Publishing.

Edmonds, H.G. (1951). *The Negro and fusion politics in North Carolina, 1894-1901.* Chapel Hill, NC: University of North Carolina Press.

Effron, S. (1990, Oct. 25) Helms, Gantt use campaign speech to reach voters. *Greensboro Newsstand Record.*

Elder, C.D. & Cobb, R.W. (1983). *The political uses of symbols.* New York: Longman.

Emery, E. & Emery, M. (1978). *The press and America.* Englewood Cliffs, NJ: Prentice-Hall.

Entman, R.M. (199). Modern racism and the images of blacks in local television news. *Critical Studies in Mass Communication,* 7(4), 332-345.

Entman, R.M. (1992). Blacks in the news: Television, modern racism and cultural change. *Journalism Quarterly,* 69(2), 341-361.

Farnsworth, D. (1963). *Farnsworth-Munsell 100 hue and dichotomous test for colorvision. Journal of Optical Society of America,* 33:18.

Fergurson, Ernest, B. (1986). *Hard rights: the rise of Jesse Helms.* New York: WW Norton.

Findahl, O. & Hoijer, B. (1981). Studies of news from the perspective of human communications. In G.C. Wilhoit and H. DeBock (eds.) *Mass Communication Review Yearbook,* Vol. 11, pp. 393-403.

Fisher, M. The KWFC index concept: A retrospective view. *American Documentation,* 17:57-70, April 1966.

Fishman, M. (1980). *Manufacturing the news.* Austin, TX: University of Texas Press.

Flemming, J.G. The Negro in American politics: The past. In *The American Negro Reference Book,* 1966.

Foner, E. (1970). *America's black past: a reader in Afro-American history*. New York: Harper and Row.

Foner, E. (1988). *Reconstructing America's unfinished revolution, 1863-1877*. New York: Harper and Row Publishers.

Forgus, R.H. & Melamed, L.E. (1976). *Perception*. 2nd ed. ., New York: McGraw-Hill.

Franklin, J. H. (1943). *The free Negro in North Carolina, 1790-1860*. Chapel Hill, NC: University of North Carolina Press.

Fromm, E. (1947). *Man for himself*. New York: Holt, Rinehart, and Winston.

Gandy, O.H., Jr. (1982). *Beyond agenda-setting: Information Subsidies and Public Policy*. Norward, NJ: Abex.

Gandy, O. (1987). "The political economy of communications competence." In. V. Mosco and J. Wasko (Eds.), *The Political Economy of Information*. Norwood, NJ: Ablex.

Gandy, O. & Coleman, L. (1986). "The Jackson campaign: Mass media and black students' perceptions." *Journalism Quarterly*, 63(1):138-143, 154.

Gandy, O.H., Jr. & Coleman, L.G. (1984). *"Watch Jesse run and tell me what you see: A first look at students' perceptions of the Jesse Jackson presidential candidacy."* Paper presented to the Minorities and Communication Division of the Association for Education in Journalism and Mass Communication. Gainesville, FL.

Gans, H.J. (1979). *Deciding what's news*. New York: Vintage Books.

Gatewood, W.B. (1975). *Black Americans and the White Man's burden, 1898-1903*. The Chicago, IL: University of Illinois Press.

Geller, A.D., Kaplan & Lasswell, H.D. (1942). An experimental comparison of four ways of coding editorial content. *Journalism Quarterly*, 19:362-370.

Gosnell, H.F. (1935). *Negro politicians.* Chicago, IL: The University of Chicago Press.

Graber, D.A. (1990). Media power in politics. *Congressional Quarterly.* Washington, D.C.

Graber, D.A. (1984). *Processing the news: how people tame the information tide.* New York: Longman.

Graber, D.A. (1980). Mass media and American politics. Washington, DC: Congressional Quarterly Press.

Gramsci, A. (1983). *The modern prince and other writings.* New York: International Publishers.

Gramsci, A. (1971). *Selections from the prison notebooks.* London: Lawrence and Wishart.

Gray, H. (1989). Television, black Americans and the American dream. *Critical Studies in Mass Communication*, 6, 376-386.

Guillory, F. (1990, Nov. 7) Late assault by Helms swayed enough voters. *The News and Observer*, p. 1A.

Hacker, A. (1992). *Two nations: black and white, separate, hostile, unequal.* New York: Charles Scribner's Sons.

Hackett, R.A. (1984). Decline of a paradigm: Bias and objectivity in news media studies. *Critical Studies in Mass Communication*, 3, 229-259.

Halberstam, D. (1988). "The southern difference: In the eye of the storm: The south in 1955." In Dudley Clendinen (ed.). *The prevailing south: life and politics in a changing culture*, pp. 28-45. Marietta, GA: Longstreet Press.

Hall, S. (1982). The rediscovery of ideology: Return of the repressed in media studies. In M. Gurevitch, T. Bennett, J. Curran, & J. Woollacott (Eds.), *Culture, Society and the Media* (pp. 56-90). London: Methuen.

Hall, S. (1980). Encoding/decoding. In S. Hall, D. Hobson, A. Lowe, & P. Willis (Eds.), *Culture, Media, Language* (pp. 128-138). London: Hutchinson.

Hall, S. (1977). Culture, the media and the ideological effect. In J. Curran, M. Gurevitch, & J. Woollacott (Eds.), *Mass Communication and Society* (pp. 315-348). London: Open University.

Hall, S., Critcher, C., Jefferson, T., Clarke, J., & Roberts, B. (1978). *Policing the Crisis: Mugging, the State and Law-and-order.* New York: Holmes and Meier.

Hampton, H. & Fayer, S. (1990). *Voices of freedom: an oral history of the civil rights movement from the 1950's through the 1980's.* New York: Blackside.

Handy, R. (1970). *The measurement of values.* St. Louis, MO: Warren H. Green.

Hanes, W. Jr. (1972). *Black politics.* New York: J.B. Lippincott.

Hartley, J. (1982). *Understanding news.* London: Methuen.

Hartmann, P., & Husband, C. (1974). *Racism and the mass media.* Totowa, NJ: Rowman and Littlefield

Hayakawa, S.F. (1972). *Language in thought and action.* 3rd ed., New York: Harcourt Brace Jovanovich.

Head, S.W. & Sterling, C.H. (1987). *Broadcasting in media.* Boston, MA: Houghton Mifflin.

Hess, S. (1986). *The ultimate insiders: U.S. senators in the national media.* Washington, DC: The Brookings Institution.

111

Hilgard, E.R., & Bowey, C.H. (1957). *Theories of learning.* Englewood Cliffs, NJ: Prentice-Hall.

Holsti, O.R An adaptation of the general inquirer for the systematic analysis of political documents. *Behavioral Science*, 9:382-88, Oct. 1964.

Holsti, O,R. (1969). *Content analysis for the social sciences and humanities.* Reading, MA: Addison Wesley.

Howard, C.I., Janis, I.L. & Kelly, H.H. (1953). *Communications and persuasion.* New Haven, CT: Yale University Press.

http://census.state.nc.us

http://quickfacts.census.gov

Iyengar, S. & Kinder, D.R. (1987). *News that matters: agenda-setting and priming in a television age.* Chicago: University of Chicago Press.

Jacob, P. (1962). *Functions of values in making policy decisions.* American Behavioral Science, 5(9):28-38.

Jamieson, K. H. (1972). *Dirty politics: deception, distraction, and democracy.* New York: Oxford University Press.

Jennings, P. (1987). *The 1986 Joe Alex Morris Jr. Memorial Lecture.* Nieman Reports, (Summer), pp. 4-9.

Kelly, T. (1983). *The imperial post.* New York: William Morrow.

Kerlinger, F.N. (1986). *Foundations of behavioral research.* New York: Holt, Rinehart, and Winston.

Kersye, M.M. & Coble, R. (1989). *North Carolina focus: an anthology on state government politics and policy.* Raleigh, NC: Publications Unlimited.

Kluckhohn, C. (1951). *Values and value orientations in the theory of action.* In T. Parsons and E.A. Chills, (ed.), Toward a General Theory of Action. Cambridge: MA: Harvard University Press.

Kluger, R, (1976). *Simple justice: the history of Brown vs. board of education and black America's struggle for equality.* New York: Alfred Knopf.

Knapp, T.J. (1986). *Approaches to cognition: contrasts and controversies.* Hilldale: NJ: Lawrence E R L Baum Associates.

Koffka, K. (1935). Principles of Gestalt psychology. New York: Harcourt Publishers.

Kraus, S. & Davis, D. *The effects of mass communication on political behavior.* Pennsylvania: The Pennsylvania State University Press.

Krech, S. & Crutchfield, R.S. (1948). *Theory and problems in social psychology.* New York: McGraw-Hill.

Krippendorff, K. (1980). *Content analysis: An introduction to its methodology.* Beverly Hills, CA: Sage Publications.

Lang, K., & Lang, G.E. (1981). Watergate: An exploration of the agenda setting process. In G.C. Wilhoit and H. DeBock (eds.) *Mass Communication Review Yearbook,* Vol. 2, pp. 447-468.

LaPiere, R.T. (1934). Attitudes vs. actions. *Social Forces,* 13:230-237.

Lasswell, H.D. et al. (1965). *Language of politics: studies in quantitative semantics.* Cambridge, MA: MIT Press.

Laurakas, P.J., Traugott, M.W. & Miller, P.V. (1995). *Presidential polls and the news media.* Oxford: Westview Press.

Leland, E. (1990, Oct. 23). Helms keeping tabs on gay's contributions: Gantt says criticism is an appeal to fears. *The Charlotte Observer* .

113

Leland, E. & Morrill, J. (1990, Oct. 27). "Gantt lashes out at secret campaign." *The Charlotte Observer.*

Lewin, K. (1941). *Human Relations.* In W. Schramm, (ed.) *Mass media and national development,* 1964, Stanford, CA: Stanford University Press.

Linsky, M. (1986). *Impact: how the press affects federal policy making.* New York: W.W. Norton.

Lippmann, W. (1922). Public opinion. Macmillan (Reprint 1965). New York: Free Press.

Littlejohn, S.W. (1983). *Theories of human communication.* Belmont, CA: Wadsworth.

Luebke, P. (1990). *Tarheel politics: myths and realities.* Chapel Hill, NC: The University of North Carolina Press.

MacGregor, M., Jr. (1981). *Integration of the Armed Forces, 1940-1965.* Washington, DC: Center of Military History, U.S. Army.

Manheim, K.B. (1987). A model of agenda dynamics. *Political communications.* Department of Political Science, Virginia Polytechnic Institute, Blacksburg, VA.

Maslow, A. (1959). *New knowledge in human values.* New York: Harper and Brothers Publishers.

Matabane, P.W. & Gandy, O.A. Jr. (1988) Through the prism of race and controversy: Did viewers learn anything from the Africans?. *Journal of Black Studies,* Vol. 19, No. 1, 3-16.

McBurney, D.H., & Collins, V.B. (1977). *Introduction of sensation and perception.* Englewood Cliffs: NJ: Prentice Hall.

McCombs, M.E. & Shaw, D.L. (1977). *The emergence of American political issues: The agenda-setting function of the press.* St. Paul: West Publishing Company.

McCombs, M.E. & Shaw, D.L. (1976). Structuring the unseen environment. *Journal of Communication,* 26, 18-22.

McCombs, M.E. & Shaw, D.L. (1972). The agenda setting function of the mass media. *Public Opinion Quarterly,* 36, 176-187.

McCombs, M.E. & Shaw D.L. (1969). *Acquiring political information.* Chapel Hill, NC: University of North Carolina Press.

McConahay, J.B. (1982). Self-interest versus racial attitudes as correlates of anti-busing attitudes in Louisville: Is it the buses or the blacks? *Journal of Politics,* 44(3), 692-720.

McConahay, J.B. (1986). Modern racism, ambivalence, and the modern racism scale. In J. Dovidio & S. Gaertner (Eds.), *Prejudice, discrimination and racism* (pp. 91-125). New York: Academic Press.

McDonald, D. Is objectivity possible? *The Center Magazine.* Sept. and Oct. 1971, p. 29.

McLuhan, H.M. (1964). *Understanding media: The extension of man.* 1st ed. New York: McGraw Hill.

Megwa, E.R. (1989). *Pressures for change: African American news sources and the news media.* Paper presented at the One-Third of A Nation African American Perspectives Conference, Howard University, Washington, D.C.

Megwa, E. R. & Brenner, D. (1989). *News from somewhere: A study of source agenda setting.* Department of Communication Arts and Sciences, School of Communications, Unpublished doctoral dissertation, Howard University, Washington, D.C.

Megwa, E.R. & Brenner, B. (1988). Toward a paradigm of media agenda setting effect: Agenda setting as a process. *The Howard Journal of Communications,* Volume I, No. 1, Spring pg. 39.

Megwa E.R & Barber, J. T. (1990). Can minority news sources set the agenda of mainstream media? Congressional black caucus and the national media. Howard University, Washington, DC.

Meier, A. & Rudwick, E. M. (1966). *From plantation to ghetto: an interpretive history of American Negroes*. New York: Hill and Wang.

Mencher, M. (1984). *News reporting and writing*. Dubuque, IA: W.C. Brown Publisher.

Merrill, J.C. How *Time* stereotyped three U.S. presidents. *Journalism Quarterly*, 42:563-570.

Merrill, J.C. & Jacks, O. (1983). *Philosophy and journalism*. New York: Longman.

Merron, J. & Gaddy, G.D. Editorial endorsement and newsplay: Bias in coverage of Ferraro's finances. *Journalism Quarterly*, 63:127-137.

Miller, S.H. (1974). News coverage of congress: Search for the ultimate spokesman. *Journalism Quarterly*, 54, 459-465.

Miller, S.H. (1978). Reporters and congressmen: Living in symbiosis. *Journalism Monographs*, 53.

Montagu, A. (1974). *Man's most dangerous myth: The fallacy of race*. London: Oxford University Press.

Moore, B.L. (1991). African-American women in the U.S. military. *Armed Forces and Society*, 17(3), 363-384.

Morrill, J. (1990, Oct. 20) Poll: Gantt leading 49% - 41%: Congress' image may affect gap; Some doubt it's that big. *The Charlotte Observer*.

Morrill, J. (1990, Oct 20) Wilder factor has sent wrong signals to pollsters before. *The Charlotte Observer*.

Morrill, J. & Drescher, J. (1990, Oct. 31) Senate language heats up: With week to go, harsh words fly. *The Charlotte Observer.*

Mosely, S.A. (Ph.D.). (1989). Poverty, politics and political transformation in North Carolina: A comparative case study of three cities. Unpublished doctoral dissertation, Ohio State University, Columbus.

Mueller, C. (1973). *The Politics of Communication: A Study in Political Sociology of Language, Socialization, and Legitimization.* New York: Oxford University Press.

Myrdal, G. (1964). *An American Dilemma: The Negro in a White Nation* (Vol. 1). New York: McGraw-Hill.

Newby, I. A. (1973). *Black Carolinians: a History of Blacks in South Carolina from 1895 to 1968.* Columbia, SC: University of South Carolina Press.

Odum, H.W. (1993). *Race and rumors of race challenge to American crisis.* Chapel Hill, NC: The University of North Carolina Press.

Osgood, C.E., Suci, G.J. & Tannenbaum, P.H. (1957). *The measurement of meaning.* Urbana: University of Illinois Press.

Osofsky, G. (1967). *The burden of race: documentary history of Negro-White relations in America.* New York: Harper and Row Publishers.

Paletz, D.L. & Entman, R.M. (1981). *Media power politics.* New York: Free Press.

Parenti, M. (1986). *Inventing reality: the politics of the mass media.* New York: St. Martin's Press.

Parker, D.H. (1968). *The philosophy of value.* New York: Greenwood Press.

Patterson, T. & McClure, R. (1976). *The unseeing eye.* New York: G.P. Putnam's.

Poindexter, P. & Stroman, C. (1981). Blacks and television: a review of the literature. *Journal of Broadcasting,* 25(2), 103-122.

Powell, W.S. *North Carolina through four centuries.* (1989). Chapel Hill, NC: University of North Carolina Press

Rawley, J.A. (1969). *Race and politics.* New York: J.B. Lippincott.

Reed, A.L. Jr. (1986). *The Jesse Jackson phenomenon.* New Haven, CT: Yale University Press.

Riley, S. (1990, Oct. 31) Gantt, Helms keep attacks at a fast boil: Democrat cities 'lies' by foe. *The News and Observer.*

Rivers, W.L. (1970). *Appraising press coverage of politics.* In Lee (ed.) *Politics and the Press.* Washington, DC: Acropolis.

Roberts, C.M. (1977). *The Washington Post: the first 100 years.* Boston: Houghton Mifflin.

Rock, I. (1983). *The Logic of Perception.* Cambridge, MA: The MIT Press.

Rogers, E.M. (1983). *Diffusion of Innovations,* 3rd ed. New York: The Free Press.

Rokeach, M. (1968). *Beliefs, attitudes, and values.* New York: The Free Press.

Rokeach, M. (1960). *The open and closed mind.* New York: Basic Books.

Robinson, J.P. & Levy, M.R. (1986). *The main source: learning from television news.* Beverly Hills, CA: Sage.

Rogers, E. & Dearing, J.W. (1986). Agenda-setting research: Where has it been, where is it going? *Communication Yearbook*, 11, pp. 555–594.

Rowan, C.T. (1976, February). Is there a conspiracy against Black leaders? *Ebony*, pp. 33–57.

Sabato, L. (1981). *The Rise of the Political Consultants: New Ways of Winning Elections*. New York: Basic Books.

Salwen, M.B. & Stacks, D.W. (1996). *An integrated approach to communication theory and research*. Mahwah, NJ: Lawrence Erlbaum Associate.

Schiller, D. (1981). *Objectivity and the News*. Philadelphia, PA: University of Pennsylvania Press.

Scholsser, J. Blacks develop voting clout. *Greensboro Record*, June 1, 1979.

Schramm, W. (1964). The flow of information in the world. In *Mass Media and National Development*, Stanford, CA: Stanford University Press.

Schudson, M. (1978). *Discovering the News: A Social History of American Newspapers*. New York: Basic Books.

Schuman, H., Steeh, C., & Bobo, L. (1985). *Racial attitudes in America: trends and interpretations*. Cambridge, MA: Harvard University Press.

Schwartzman, E. (1984). *Political campaign craftsmanship: a professional's candid guide to campaigning for public office*. New York: Vannostrand Reinhold.

Sears, D.O. (1988). Symbolic Racism. In P.A. Katz & D.A. Taylor (Eds.), *Eliminating racism* (pp. 53–84). New York: Plenum Press.

Severin, W.J. & Tankard, J.W. Jr. (1979). *Communication theories.* New York: Hasting House.

Shah, H., & Thornton, M.C. (1994). Racial ideology in U.S. mainstream news magazine coverage of black-latino interaction, 1980-1992. *Critical Studies in Mass Communication*, 11(2), 141-161.

Shaw, D. (1981). News bias and the telegraph: Study of historical change. *Journalism Quarterly*, 44:3-12, 31.

Shaw, D.L. (1981). At the crossroads: Change and continuity in American press news 1820-1860. *Journalism History*, Summer 8:2, 38-50 .

Sherif, C.W., & M. Sherif. (1967). *Attitudes, ego involvement, and change.* New York: John Wiley and Sons.

Sherif, C.W., M. Sherif, and R.E. Nebergall. (1965). *Attitudes and attitude change: the social judgment involvement, and change.* New York: John Wiley and Son.

Sherif, M. (1948). *Outline of social psychology.* New York: Harper Brothers Publishers.

Sherif, M. & Sherif, C.W. (1954). *Social psychology.* New York: John Wiley and Sons.

Sherif, M., & H.C. (1947). *The psychology of ego involvement.* New York: John Wiley and Sons.

Siebert, F.S., Peterson, T. & Schramm, W. (1976). The Libertarian theory of the press. In *Four theories of the press.* Urbana, IL: University of Illinois Press.

Siebert, F.S., Peterson, T. & Schramm, W. (1956). *Four theories of the press.* Urbana, IL: University of Illinois Press.

Snider, W.D. (1985). *Helms and Hunt: the North Carolina senate race, 1984.* Chapel Hill, NC: The University of North Carolina Press.

Stempel, G.H., III. & Westley, B.H. (1981). *Research methods in mass communication.* Englewood Cliffs, NJ: Prentice Hall.

Stevenson, R.L. & Greene, M.T. (1980). A reconsideration of bias in the news. *Journalism Quarterly,* 57:115.

Stone, C. (1970). *Black political power in America.* New York: Bobbs Merrill.

Stone, P. et. a1. (1966). *The general inquirer: a computer approach to content analysis.* Cambridge, MA: MPT Press.

Tan, A. (1981). *Mass communication theories and research.* Columbus, OH: Grid Publishing.

Tate, K. (1993). *From protest to politics: the new black voters in American elections.* New York: Russell Sage Foundation.

Tipton, L., Haney, R. & Basehart, J. (1975). Media agenda setting in city and state election campaigns. *Journalism Quarterly.* 52(1), pp. 15-22.

Truman, H.S. (1948). *Text of executive order 9981.* Washington, DC: U.S. Government.

Tuchman, G. (1978). *Making news: a study in the construction of reality.* New York: MacMillan.

Turk, J.V. (1986). Information subsidies and media content: A study of pubic relations influence on the news. *Journalism Monograph,* No. 100.

Van Dijk, T. (1991). *Racism and the press.* New York: Routledge.

Vandergrift, Paul F., Jr. (1987). *Use of telecommunication as a teaching strategy: Perceptions of top administrators in North Carolina community college system,* Dissertation. North Carolina State University, Raleigh.

Vander Zander, J.W. (1970). *Sociology: systematic approach.* New York: Ronald Press.

Vermeer, J.P. (1987). *Campaigns in the news: mass media and congressional elections.* New York: Greenwood Press.

Walker, J.L. (1977). Setting the agenda in the U.S. Senate: a theory of problem selection. *British Journal of Political Science,* 7:433-445.

Weaver D.H. (1984). Media agenda setting and public opinion: is there a link? *Communication Yearbook,* Vol. 18, pp. 680-691.

Weaver, D.H. & Elliott, S.N. (1985). Who set the agenda for the media? A study of local agenda-building. A paper presented at the Association for Education in Journalism and Mass Communication, Gainesville, FL.

Weaver, D.H. & Wilhoit, G.C. (1980). News media coverage of U.S. Senators in four congresses, 1953-1974. *Journalism Monographs,* 67, 1-34.

Weaver, D.H., & G.C. Wilhoit. (1986). *The American journalist,* Bloomington, IN: University Press.

West, Cornel. (1993). *Race Matters.* Boston, MA: Beacon Press.

White, D.M. (1950). "The gatekeeper: A case study in the selection of news." *Journalism Quarterly,* 26, 383-390.

Whiteside, T. Corridor of mirrors. *Columbia Journalism Review.* Winter, 1968-69, pp. 33-54.

Williams, J. (1985). Redefining institutional racism. *Ethnic and Racial Studies,* 8(3), 323-348.

Wilhoit, G.C. & Sherill, K.S. (1968). Wire service visibility of U.S. Senators. *Journalism Quarterly,* 45, 43-47.

Wireback, T. (1990, Oct. 21) "Senate race: Two very public men fight for starbilling: home Helms happy in midst of controversy." *Greensboro News and Records.*

Woodward, C. V. (1988). "The southern difference: the particular politics of being southern. In Dudley Clendinen (ed.). *The prevailing south: life and politics in a changing culture,* pp. 16027. Marietta, GA: Longstreet Press.

World Almanac and Book of Facts. (2006) New York: WRC Media Group.

www.ncleg.net/legislativelibrary/historicalinfo.

www.u.s.census.americanfactfinder.

Znaniecki, F. (1952). Should sociologists be also philosophers of values? *Social Research,* 37:79-84.

Zimbardo, P. & Ebgeson, E.B. (1969). *Influencing attitudes and changing behavior.* Menlo Park, CA: Addison-Wesley Publishing Company.

CPSIA information can be obtained at www.ICGtesting.com
Printed in the USA
LVOW11*1815140314

377471LV00002B/26/P